Contents

Age-Appropriate Skills

Language

- following directions
- story comprehension
- descriptive and comparative language
- rhyming
- categorization
- letter and sound recognition
- statements and questions
- auditory and visual memory
- left to right tracking
- oral language
- vocabulary and concept development
- sequencing
- color words

Math

- counting to 20
- patterning
- numeral recognition
- geometric shapes
- ordinal numbers
- beginning computation
- one-to-one matching
- graphing
- measurement

Circle-Time Books

Making Circle-Time Books

Follow these simple directions to assemble a circle-time book for each of the five sections of *Animals Around the World.*

- Tear out and laminate the color story pages for each circle-time book.

- Bind the books with binder rings or an alternative binding method.

- Read the circle-time book as the opening activity for each section of *Animals Around the World.*

Place the book on an easel or chalkboard stand and flip the pages for easy reading.

Sharing Circle-Time Books

Each circle-time story introduces the topic of that section. Begin by reading the story to the children several times. The first time you read it, you might ask children to predict what the story will be about by looking at the cover illustration. In subsequent readings, use strategies such as:

- moving your finger under words as you read to model left to right tracking

- allowing children to "read" the predictable text

- asking children to identify objects in the pictures

- talking about any rhyming words

- asking children to predict what will happen next in the story

- asking questions to help children recall story details

- asking at least one question that relates to children's own lives

Circle-Time Books

Section One
Animals of the Savanna

"Animals of the Savanna" (pages 13–22)
Use this colorful book to introduce children to some of the animals that live on the savanna. Pause on each page and discuss the illustrations. Allow children to share what they know about animals that live on the savanna. Explain to children that they will learn about parent animals and baby animals that live on the savanna. They will also learn about some of their behaviors.

Ask questions such as:

- What does the savanna look like?
- What are the lion and its cubs doing?
- What is one thing that makes a giraffe different from other animals?
- How do the elephant and its calf stay cool?
- What do hippos eat?
- What do zebras eat?
- Do ostriches run fast or slow?

Section Two
Animals of the Forest

"Animals of the Forest" (pages 51–60)
This story introduces children to many of the animals that live in the forest. The story highlights some typical animal behaviors. As you read children the story, draw their attention to the forest environment. Point out the tall trees and short bushes. Point out the animals and plants in and around the lake. Talk about where the animals in the forest may live.

Ask questions such as:

- What are the robins using to build their nest?
- Where are the spotted salamanders?
- What is the bear getting out of the tree? Which type of insect is he disturbing?
- Where are the moose eating waterlilies?
- What is the beaver using to build a dam?
- How do you think the dew got on the leaves?

Section Three
Animals of the Desert

"Animals of the Desert" (pages 89–98)
Use this colorful book to introduce children to some of the animals that live in the desert. Pause on each page and allow children to point out some of the characteristics of a desert environment. Allow children to share what they know about a desert environment. Ask them if they think the desert is hot or cold. Ask children if they have ever seen any desert animals up close.

Ask questions such as:

- What does the bobcat do at night?
- Does a roadrunner run fast?
- Do coyotes hunt alone or together?
- Is a rattlesnake dangerous? Why is it called a rattlesnake?
- What does a desert iguana eat?
- How does a kangaroo rat move?

3

Circle-Time Books

Section Four
Animals of the Arctic Tundra

"Animals of the Arctic Tundra" (pages 127–136)
This rhyming story introduces children to animals that live in the arctic tundra. As you read the story, pause on each page and ask children to identify the rhyming words. Point out different characteristics of the arctic tundra. Ask children if they notice anything that the animals have in common.

Ask questions such as:

- What does an arctic fox look like?

- What color is an arctic hare? What is another name for "hare"?

- When does the snowy owl hunt?

- Which sea are the seals swimming in?

- What do caribou use to "shovel" snow?

- What does the walrus use to help it climb out of the sea?

Section Five
Animals of the Rainforest

"Animals of the Rainforest" (pages 161–170)
This story uses simple rhyme to introduce children to some of the animals living in the rainforest. As you read the story, pause on each page and ask children to identify the rhyming words. Point out the different places that animals spend time in the forest. Point out that there is a lot of plant life in the rainforest. Allow children to share what they know about the rainforest.

Ask questions such as:

- What is the anteater looking for?

- Where is the jaguar standing? How many colors is the jaguar?

- Does the sloth move fast or slow?

- How does the spider monkey move through the trees?

- What colors are on the toucan's beak?

Take-Home Books

Use these simple directions to make reproducible take-home books for each of the five sections of *Animals Around the World*.

1. Reproduce the book pages for each child.

2. Cut the pages along the cut lines.

3. Place the pages in order, or this may be done as a sequencing activity with children. Guide children in assembling the book page by page.

4. Staple the book together.

After making each take-home book, review the story as children turn the pages of their own books. Send the storybook home along with the Parent Letter on page 5.

Dear Parent(s) or Guardian(s),

As part of our unit *Animals Around the World*, I will be presenting five storybooks to the class. Your child will receive a take-home storybook for you to share. Remember that reading to children helps them develop a love of reading. Regularly reading aloud to children has proven to enhance a variety of early language skills, including:

- vocabulary and concept development,
- letter recognition,
- phonemic awareness,
- auditory and visual discrimination, and
- left to right tracking.

I hope you enjoy sharing these stories with your child.

As you read to your child, remember to:

1. speak clearly and with interest.
2. track words by moving your finger under each word as you read it.
3. ask your child to help you identify objects in the pictures. Talk about these objects together.
4. discuss your own experiences as they relate to the story.
5. allow your child to express his or her own thoughts and ideas and to ask you questions.

I hope you enjoy all five of the animal stories.

Sincerely,

_____

Storyboards

A storyboard is an excellent way to enhance vocabulary and concept development.

Each section of *Animals Around the World* includes full-color storyboard pieces to use in extending the language and concepts introduced. Ideas for using the storyboard pieces in each section are found on pages 7–9.

Turn the full-color cutouts into pieces that will adhere to a flannel- or felt-covered storyboard. Just laminate the pieces and affix self-sticking Velcro® dots to the back of each piece.

Animals of the Savanna
pages 29 and 31

Animals of the Forest
pages 67–71

Animals of the Desert
pages 105 and 107

Animals of the Arctic Tundra
pages 143 and 145

Animals of the Rainforest
pages 177 and 179

Storyboards

"Animals of the Savanna" Storyboard Use the colorful storyboard pieces on pages 29 and 31 to follow up your presentation of the story "Animals of the Savanna." You may choose to use the following teacher script to present the story:

> *Today we are going to put together our own savanna animal storyboard. I am going to show you animal babies and parents that live on the savanna. We will talk about them.*
>
> *Here are some animals you might recognize. Here is a lion and its cubs. They play with each other. They lie next to each other in the tall grass. Here is a giraffe with its calf. They stretch their long necks up to the trees. They like to eat acacia leaves. Here is an elephant with its calf. They use their trunks to suck up water.*
>
> *Here is a hippo with its calf. The mother hippo gives her calf a ride on her back. Here is a zebra with her foal. Zebras have a black-and-white striped coat.*

Remove the storyboard pieces and allow children to replace each piece as they retell the story.

"Animals of the Forest" Storyboard Use the colorful storyboard pieces on pages 67–71 to follow up your presentation of the story "Animals of the Forest." You may choose to use the following teacher script to present the story:

> *Today we are going to put together our own forest animal storyboard. I am going to show you animals that live in the forest. We will talk about them.*
>
> *Here are the robins. They are carrying sticks and leaves in their beaks. They are building a nest in the pine tree. Here are three salamanders scurrying on the forest floor. Salamanders sometimes hide in or near a log on the forest floor.*
>
> *Here is a bear. He is looking for honey. This tree has a beehive in it. The bear will climb the tree and look for honey. Here are two moose. Moose like to go to the lakes and streams in the forest. They like to eat waterlily plants. Here is a beaver. This beaver is building a dam. He slaps his tail when danger is near. Here is a deer. This deer is thirsty. It drinks by licking the dew off the leaves.*

Remove the storyboard pieces and allow children to replace each piece as they retell the story.

Storyboards

Section Three
Animals of the Desert

"Animals of the Desert" Storyboard Use the colorful storyboard pieces on pages 105 and 107 to follow up your presentation of the story "Animals of the Desert." You may choose to use the following teacher script to present the story:

> *Today we are going to put together our own desert animal storyboard. I am going to show you animals that live in the desert. We will talk about them.*
>
> *Here is a bobcat. It is sleeping. The bobcat will wake up at night and hunt for food. Here is a roadrunner. Does the roadrunner fly or run across the sand? Does a roadrunner move quickly or slowly?*
> *Here is a pack of coyotes. They roam through the desert during the day. Coyotes also sleep during the day. What do they do at night?*
> *Here is a rattlesnake. It likes to slither up onto a desert rock.*
> *Here is a desert iguana. It likes to eat desert flowers.*
> *Here is a kangaroo rat. Its long legs help it to jump high.*

Remove the storyboard pieces and allow children to replace each piece as they retell the story.

Section Four
Animals of the Arctic Tundra

"Animals of the Arctic Tundra" Storyboard Use the colorful storyboard pieces on pages 143 and 145 to follow up your presentation of the story "Animals of the Arctic Tundra." You may choose to use the following teacher script to present the story:

> *Today we are going to put together our own arctic tundra animal storyboard. I am going to show you animals that live in the arctic tundra. We will talk about them.*
>
> *Here is an arctic fox. It is sleeping curled in a ball. It has a bushy tail. Here is another arctic fox. It is looking for food. Here is an arctic hare. It is white. If you put it on the snow it is hard to see because it is camouflaged. Here is a snowy owl. It has yellow eyes. It flies through the arctic skies. Here is a seal. It likes to slide across the ice. Here is a caribou. It is using its antlers to shovel the snow. It is looking for the green growth under the snow. Here is a walrus in the water. It is using its tusks to pull itself out of the water.*

Remove the storyboard pieces and allow children to replace each piece as they retell the story.

"Animals of the Rainforest" Storyboard Use the colorful storyboard pieces on pages 177 and 179 to follow up your presentation of the story "Animals of the Rainforest." You may choose to use the following teacher script to present the story:

Today we are going to put together our own rainforest animal storyboard. I am going to show you animals that live in the rainforest. We will talk about them.

Here is a sloth hanging from a tree. Sloths move very slowly. Here is a jaguar sitting on a branch. Look at the jaguar's pattern. Here is a harpy eagle flying through the trees. It is watching the ground from above. Here is a giant anteater climbing on a tree. It is looking for ants to eat. It sticks out its long tongue to catch the ants. Here is a toucan. How many colors can you see? Here is a spider monkey. It uses it arms, legs, and tail to swing from tree to tree. It has two colors on its fur. What are they?

Remove the storyboard pieces and allow children to replace each piece as they retell the story.

Creating an Atmosphere

Build concepts by creating a bulletin board that displays animals in their different habitats.

Make an Animals Around the World Bulletin Board

• Staple blue butcher paper on the board for a backing.

• Use construction paper or butcher paper, depending upon the size of your bulletin board area. Add details with a marking pen.

• Make a habitat model for each of the four habitats. Cut landscape backgrounds such as grass, trees, snow, and sand.

• Add appropriate animals and plants to each habitat area by following the simple directions on page 11.

Simple Steps to Show You How

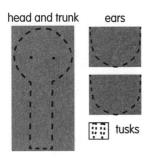

head and trunk   ears

tusks

Savanna

- Use yellow paper for the background. Fringe one side of a strip of green paper for grass.
- Cut an elephant head from gray and white paper. Add details with a marker.
- Label the section with large cutout letters.

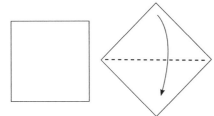

fold behind

Arctic Tundra

- Use blue paper for the background. Cut peaks along one side of a strip of white paper to make the snow.
- Fold a white paper square to make an arctic fox. Add details with a marker.
- Label the section with large cutout letters.

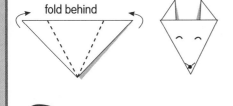

Desert

- Use orange paper for the background. Cut one side of a strip of yellow or tan paper for the sand.
- Cut a snake from a brown piece of paper. Add details with a marker and colored pencils. Fold and curl the snake and staple it to the board.
- Cut a cactus from green paper. Add details with a marker.
- Label the section with large cutout letters.

head   paw

snout   ears

Forest

- Use white paper for the background. Cut a row of trees from green paper for the forest.
- Cut a bear from dark and light brown paper. Add details with a marker.
- Label the section with large cutout letters.

Animals of the Savanna

Children learn about some of the animals that live on the African savanna. Explain to children that a savanna can be found in many places around the world. Tell them that a savanna is an area of land that is covered by tall, dry grass and scattered trees and bushes. Explain to children that they will learn about some of the animals that live on the African savanna.

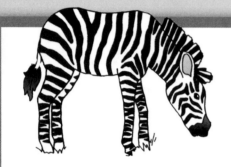

Animals of the Savanna

Take a walk through the savanna.
Follow me.
There are many animals for us to see.

See the lion and its cubs
playing and having fun.
Later, they will stretch their legs
and rest in the sun.

See the giraffe and its calf
browsing on acacia leaves.
Their long necks easily reach
into the tallest trees.

 All About Animals Around the World • EMC 2411 • ©2005 by Evan-Moor Corp.

See the elephant and its calf
flapping their ears to stay cool.
Their long trunks suck up water
from a nearby savanna pool.

See the big mother hippo
giving her calf a ride.
They will eat water plants
when they reach the other side.

See the striped zebra.
Her foal is at her side.
Eating grass all day,
they roam far and wide.

See the long-legged ostrich
and her downy chick.
When they spy danger,
they race away—they are quick!

All About Animals Around the World • EMC 2411 • ©2005 by Evan-Moor Corp.

Can you name the wild animals
we saw today?
What makes the savanna
a good place for them to stay?

The End

Note: Teachers will make copies
and cut them in half for minibooks.

Reproducible Story

Animals
of the Savanna

Take a walk through
the savanna.
Follow me.
There are many animals
for us to see.

1

See the lion and its cubs playing and having fun. Later, they will stretch their legs and rest in the sun.

2

See the giraffe and its calf browsing on acacia leaves. Their long necks easily reach into the tallest trees.

3

See the elephant
and its calf flapping
their ears to stay cool.
Their long trunks suck
up water from a nearby
savanna pool.

4

See the big mother
hippo giving her calf
a ride. They will eat
water plants when they
reach the other side.

5

See the striped zebra.
Her foal is at her side.
Eating grass all day, they
roam far and wide.

6

See the long-legged
ostrich and her
downy chick.
When they spy danger,
they race away—
they are quick!

7

Can you name the wild animals we saw today? What makes the savanna a good place for them to stay?

8

The End

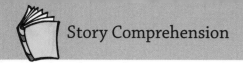 Story Comprehension

Note: Children draw a line from each animal parent to its baby.

Name _____

Savanna Families

Match. Draw a line.

Note: See page 7 for suggestions on using the storyboard pieces on pages 29 and 31 for Animals of the Savanna.

Storyboard Pieces

Animals
of the Savanna

©2005 by Evan-Moor Corp.
All About Animals Around the World • EMC 2411

Animals
of the Savanna

©2005 by Evan-Moor Corp.
All About Animals Around the World • EMC 2411

Animals
of the Savanna

©2005 by Evan-Moor Corp.
All About Animals Around the World • EMC 2411

Animals
of the Savanna

Animals
of the Savanna

Animals
of the Savanna

Children create a paper bag giraffe puppet.

Materials

- pages 34 and 35, reproduced, one per child

- lunch-size paper bags, one per child

- markers or crayons

- scissors

- glue

- Optional: plastic googly eyes

Paper Bag Giraffe

Preparation

1. Allow children to share what they know about giraffes. Tell them that giraffes have a pattern on their body. Show children a picture of a giraffe.

2. Model the steps for this project and a completed Paper Bag Giraffe.

Steps to Follow

1. Children color and cut out the patterns on pages 34 and 35. Children make cut lines up the back of the giraffe's neck.

2. Children take a paper bag and turn it upside down, making sure the flap is facing forward. They glue the giraffe's head to the flap as shown.

3. Then they glue the giraffe's body to the paper bag.

4. Children have a class giraffe puppet show.

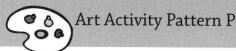

Note: Reproduce the patterns on pages 34 and 35 to use with Paper Bag Giraffe art activity.

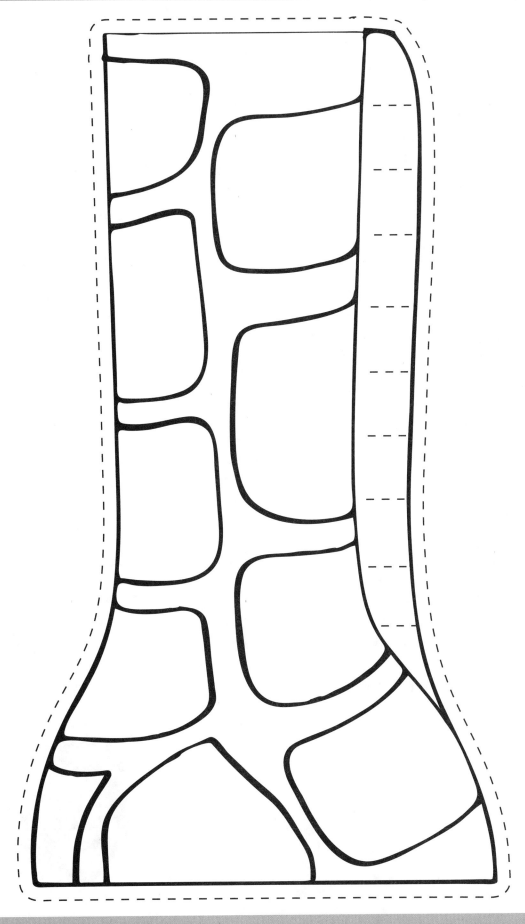

Note: Check for allergies before beginning any cooking activity. An allergic reaction can occur through taste, smell, or contact with allergens.

Camouflage Cookies

Children make cookies that are frosted in animal camouflage patterns.

Preparation

1. Cover a table with waxed paper. Place a light layer of flour on the paper.

2. Children use a dull knife to slice the cookie dough roll. Children place the cookie slices on a baking sheet. An adult bakes the cookies.

3. Spoon chocolate frosting into a bowl. Spoon some of the vanilla frosting into a bowl.

4. Children use some of the vanilla frosting and food coloring to make both yellow and black frosting.

5. Allow time for the cookies to cool before children begin frosting them.

6. Explain to children that some animals have a pattern on their skin or fur that helps hide, or camouflage, them from other animals. Ask them which colors and patterns giraffes and zebras have on their fur. Point out to children that the zebra's striped pattern makes it hard to distinguish one zebra in particular from the herd. This makes it difficult for a predator to catch a zebra.

Steps to Follow

1. Children take a cookie and use the white and the black frosting to create a zebra pattern.

2. They take a second cookie and use the yellow and the chocolate frosting to create a giraffe pattern.

3. Children discuss which other animals have camouflage patterns while eating their tasty treats!

Materials

- refrigerated sugar cookie dough (enough for two cookies per child)
- vanilla frosting
- chocolate frosting
- food coloring
- flour
- dull plastic knives
- plastic spoons
- four small bowls
- waxed paper
- spatula
- cookie sheets
- oven

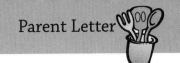

Dear Parent(s) or Guardian(s),

Today we cooked in class. Your child helped prepare "Camouflage Cookies." Besides having fun cooking and eating, the children practiced these skills:

- listening to and following directions
- vocabulary and concept development
- using small motor skills

For our unit *Animals Around the World*, we will send home a variety of new recipes. Each recipe will be one that your child has tried in class and is excited about. We hope you have an opportunity to try this recipe again with your child. Allowing your child to help you in the kitchen is a wonderful way to reinforce learning skills while creating family memories.

Camouflage Cookies

Materials

- refrigerated sugar cookie dough
- vanilla frosting
- chocolate frosting
- food coloring
- flour
- dull plastic knives
- plastic spoons
- four small bowls
- waxed paper
- spatula
- cookie sheet
- oven

Steps to Follow

1. Follow the directions on the package to bake the sugar cookies. Allow cookies to cool before frosting them.
2. Use some of the vanilla frosting and add food coloring to make it yellow.
3. Use some of the vanilla frosting and add food coloring to make it black.
4. Take a cookie and use the white and the black frosting to create a zebra pattern.
5. Take another cookie and use the yellow and the chocolate frosting to create a giraffe pattern.
6. Enjoy your Camouflage Cookies!

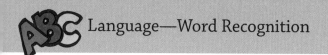
Language—Word Recognition

Note: Read the directions to the children. Explain that the lion is trying to find his cubs in the grass. Children color a path for the lion.

Name _____

Where Are My Cubs?

Help the lion find his cubs.

Color the boxes with the word **cub**.

cub	lion	grass	tree
cub	grass	tree	lion
cub	cub	cub	cub
grass	lion	tree	cub
lion	bug	grass	cub

Note: Children count the stripes on each zebra and write the number on the line.

Math—Counting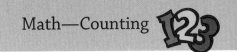

Name _____

How Many Stripes?

Count the stripes.

Write the number.

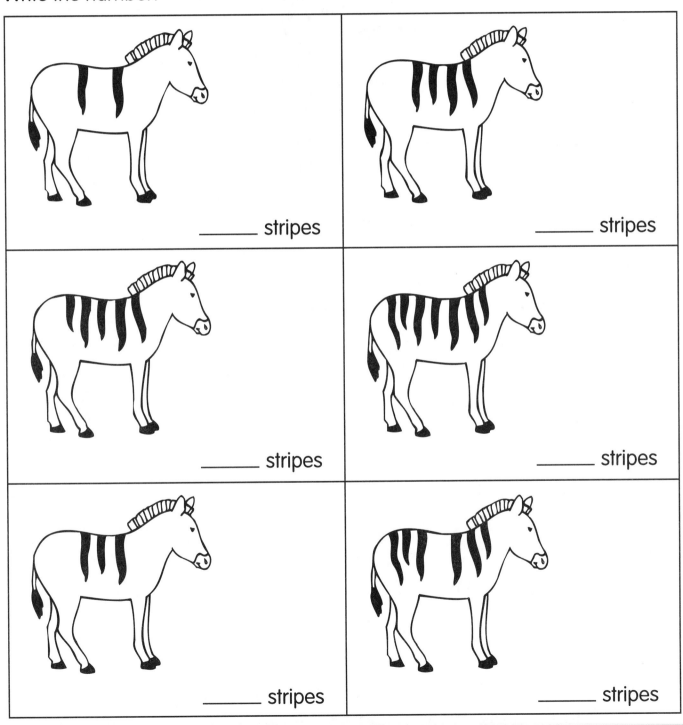

_____ stripes

_____ stripes

_____ stripes

_____ stripes

_____ stripes

_____ stripes

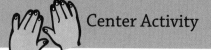

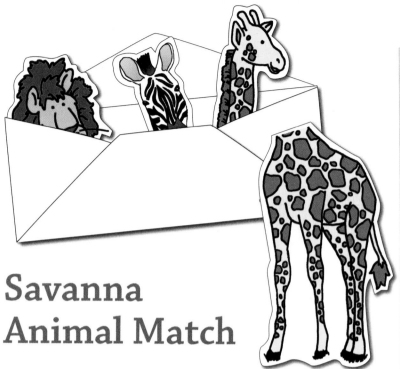

Savanna Animal Match

Creating the Center

1. Laminate and cut apart pages 41 through 45.
2. Place the animal heads and bodies in an envelope.

Using the Center

Children take the animal pieces out of the envelope and match each animal head with the correct animal body.

Children match each animal head to the correct animal body.

Materials

- pages 41–45, laminated
- scissors
- envelope

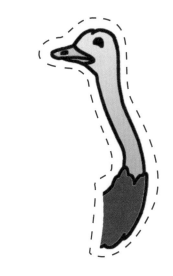

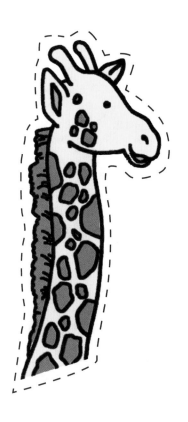

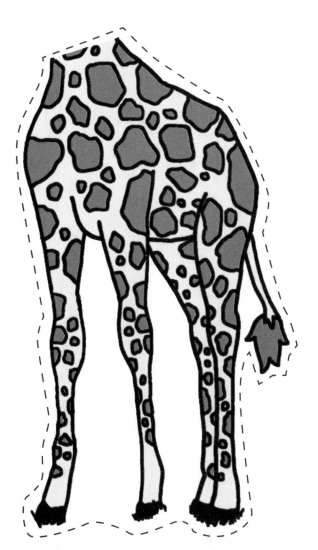

Animals of the Savanna **41**

Savanna
Animal Match

©2005 by Evan-Moor Corp.
All About Animals Around the World • EMC 2411

Savanna
Animal Match

©2005 by Evan-Moor Corp.
All About Animals Around the World • EMC 2411

Savanna
Animal Match

©2005 by Evan-Moor Corp.
All About Animals Around the World
EMC 2411

Savanna
Animal Match

©2005 by Evan-Moor Corp.
All About Animals Around the World • EMC 2411

Savanna Animal Match

Savanna
Animal Match

Savanna
Animal Match

Savanna
Animal Match

Savanna
Animal Match

©2005 by Evan-Moor Corp.
All About Animals Around the World • EMC 2411

Savanna
Animal Match

©2005 by Evan-Moor Corp.
All About Animals Around the World
EMC 2411

Savanna
Animal Match

©2005 by Evan-Moor Corp.
All About Animals Around the World • EMC 2411

Savanna
Animal Match

©2005 by Evan-Moor Corp.
All About Animals Around the World • EMC 2411

Children go on a safari and observe different savanna animals.

Safari Walk

Preparation

1. Discuss which animals live in the savanna. Model the appropriate animal sounds and movements for each animal. Talk about the types of food all the animals eat.

2. Explain to children that there will be two groups for this game. One group will pretend to be animals of the savanna, and the other group will be people on a safari.

3. Allow children to decide if they want to go on the safari or be one of the animals of the savanna.

4. Call out the animal names below. Tell children to raise their hand and go to the area you point to when they hear the animal name they want to be.

   - elephant
   - ostrich
   - lion
   - giraffe

5. Plan to play in an outdoor space.

How to Play

1. "Savanna animals" go to their specified area and make the appropriate animal sounds and movements.

2. Children on a safari walk from one animal group to the next and try to guess which animals they are seeing.

3. Once all the savanna animals have been viewed, allow the children on the safari to ask the animals questions about what they eat and where they live.

Note: Lead the children in this chant sung to the tune of "Going on a Bear Hunt." Children chant lines in italics.

Music/Dramatic Play Activity

Going to the Savanna

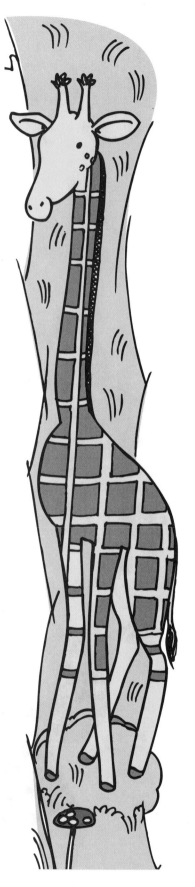

Going to the savanna.

Going to the savanna.

I'm not afraid.

I'm not afraid.

What's that up ahead?

(place open hand to forehead)

What's that up ahead?

Tall grass!

Tall grass!

Can't go over it.

Can't go over it.

Can't go under it.

Can't go under it.

Can't go around it.

Can't go around it.

Got to go through it.

(make hand motion like you are clearing a way through grass)

Got to go through it.

We're here!

We're here!

Looking for an elephant.

Looking for an elephant.

I'm not afraid.

I'm not afraid.

What's that up ahead?

(place open hand to forehead)

What's that up ahead?

An elephant!

An elephant!

Can't go over it.

Can't go over it.

Can't go around it.

Can't go around it.

Can't go through it.

Can't go through it.

Got to go under it.

(bend knees and lean back like going under a limbo stick)

Got to go under it.

Whew!

(wipe back of hand across forehead)

Whew!

Extension

Create additional verses using different savanna animals.

Savanna Animal Finger Puppets

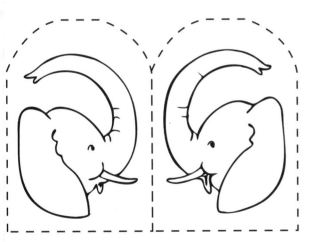

Animals of the Forest

Children learn about some of the animals that live in a forest. Explain to children that there are many forests all over the world. Tell them that a forest is an area of land that is covered by a lot of trees that grow close together. Explain to children that they will learn about some of the animals that live in a forest.

Animals of the Forest

Take a walk through the forest.
Follow me.
There are many animals for us to see.

See the robins carrying sticks and leaves.
They're building nests in the tall pine trees.

See the spotted salamander
on the damp forest floor.
Look down quick!
There go three more!

See the hungry bear reaching for a treat.
He'll poke his paw in the hive
and pull out something sweet.

See the enormous moose
grazing near the shore.
They'll eat waterlilies
until there aren't any more.

See the busy beaver building a dam.
When danger is near,
he slaps his tail—wham!

See the graceful deer drinking morning dew.
Look closely, you will see that there are two.

 All About Animals Around the World • EMC 2411 • ©2005 by Evan-Moor Corp.

Can you name the animals
we saw today?
What makes the forest
a good place for them to stay?

The End

Note: Teachers will make copies and cut in half for minibooks.

Reproducible Story

Animals
of the Forest

Take a walk through
the forest.
Follow me.
There are many animals
for us to see.

1

See the robins
carrying sticks
and leaves.
They're building
nests in the tall
pine trees.

2

See the spotted
salamander
on the damp
forest floor.
Look down quick!
There go three more!

3

See the hungry bear reaching for a treat. He'll poke his paw in the hive and pull out something sweet.

4

See the enormous moose grazing near the shore. They'll eat waterlilies until there aren't any more.

5

See the busy beaver
building a dam.
When there is danger,
he slaps his tail—wham!

6

See the graceful deer
drinking morning dew.
Look closely, you will
see that there are two.

7

Can you name the animals we saw today? What makes the forest a good place for them to stay?

8

The End

Story Comprehension

Note: Children draw a line from each animal to what it did or ate in Animals of the Forest.

Name _____

What Did I Do?

Match. Draw a line.

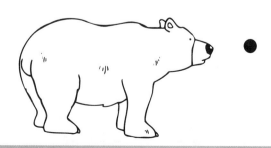

Note: See page 7 for suggestions on using the storyboard pieces on pages 67–71 for Animals of the Forest.

Storyboard Pieces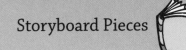

Animals
of the Forest

©2005 by Evan-Moor Corp.
All About Animals Around the World • EMC 2411

Animals
of the Forest

©2005 by Evan-Moor Corp.
All About Animals Around the World
EMC 2411

Animals
of the Forest

©2005 by Evan-Moor Corp.
All About Animals Around the World • EMC 2411

Animals
of the Forest

©2005 by Evan-Moor Corp.
All About Animals Around the World
EMC 2411

Animals
of the Forest

©2005 by Evan-Moor Corp.
All About Animals Around the World • EMC 2411

Animals
of the Forest

©2005 by Evan-Moor Corp.
All About Animals Around the World
EMC 2411

Animals
of the Forest

©2005 by Evan-Moor Corp.
All About Animals Around the World
EMC 2411

Animals
of the Forest

©2005 by Evan-Moor Corp.
All About Animals Around the World
EMC 2411

**Animals
of the Forest**

©2005 by Evan-Moor Corp.
All About Animals Around the World
EMC 2411

**Animals
of the Forest**

©2005 by Evan-Moor Corp.
All About Animals Around the World • EMC 2411

**Animals
of the Forest**

©2005 by Evan-Moor Corp.
All About Animals Around the World • EMC 2411

**Animals
of the Forest**

©2005 by Evan-Moor Corp.
All About Animals Around the World • EMC 2411

Children color, cut out, and paint a hungry bear reaching into a tree for honey.

Materials

- pages 74 and 75, reproduced, one per child
- white construction paper, one sheet per child
- green tempera paint
- sponges, cut into small rectangles
- pie tins
- scissors
- crayons or markers
- glue

Beary Hungry

Preparation

1. Cut several sponges into small rectangles. Children will use these to sponge paint a treetop.

2. Pour green tempera paint into several pie tins.

3. Plan time to model the steps for this project and a completed Beary Hungry picture.

Steps to Follow

1. Children color and cut out the tree trunk, bear, and beehive.

2. Then they glue the tree and the bear to a sheet of white construction paper, leaving enough room to sponge paint the treetop above the tree trunk.

3. Next, children dip a rectangle-shaped sponge into green paint and paint a treetop above the tree trunk.

4. Once children have completed their treetop, they set the picture aside and allow the paint to dry.

5. Once the paint has dried, children glue on the hive and draw a background scene. They may wish to add bees around the hive by drawing a yellow circle and adding black stripes, wings, and a black line for a stinger.

Art Activity Pattern Piece

Note: Reproduce the patterns on pages 74 and 75 to use with Beary Hungry art activity.

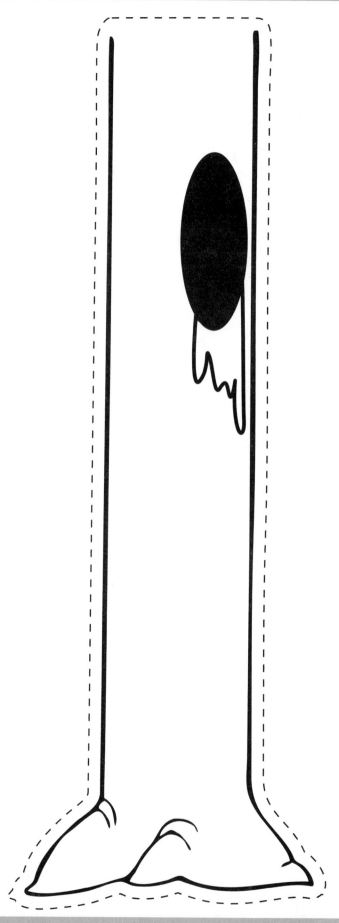

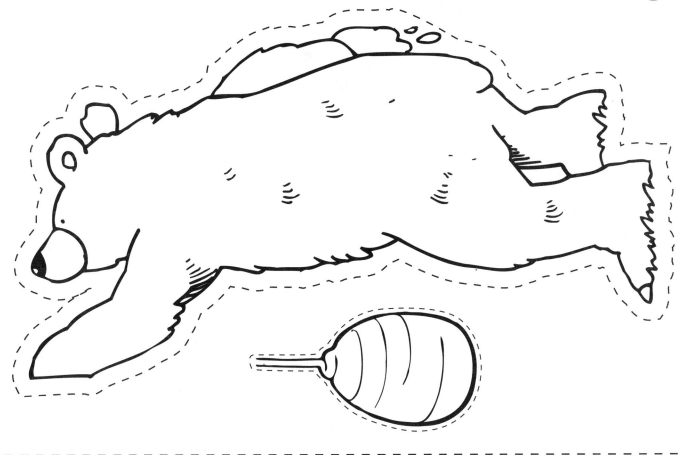

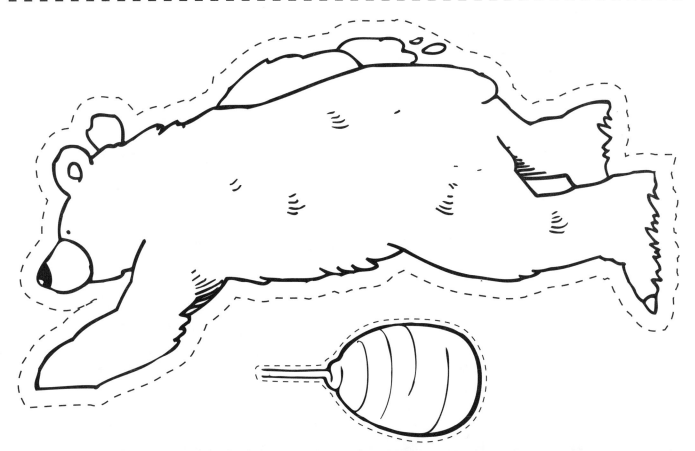

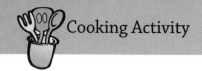

Robin's Nest

Children make a simple, tasty "robin's nest" using chocolate, butterscotch, and chow mein noodles.

Preparation

1. Explain to children that robins build a nest made of twigs and other items from the forest. Tell them that they will make a pretend robin's nest, eggs and all.

2. Plan time to model the steps for this project.

Steps to Follow

1. Children measure 1 cup (200 g) of butterscotch morsels and 1 cup (200 g) of chocolate morsels and pour each into an individual microwave-safe bowl.

2. An adult heats both bowls of morsels for one minute. Children stir the heated morsels.

3. An adult heats the morsels again for 15 to 30 seconds. Children stir the morsels. Continue to heat and stir until the morsels are just melted.

4. Children then measure 2 cups (100 g) of chow mein noodles and pour them into the bowl of melted butterscotch. Stir until the noodles are completely covered. Then they do the same with the melted chocolate.

5. Children use a large plastic spoon to scoop some butterscotch-covered and some chocolate-covered noodles onto a waxed paper square. This is the robin's nest. Then children shape the nest so it will hold "blue eggs" in the center.

6. Children add the eggs to their robin's nest.

7. Allow time for the nests to set, and enjoy!

Materials

- 11.5-oz. (326 g) bag of butterscotch morsels

- 11.5-oz. (326 g) bag of chocolate morsels

- chow mein noodles, 4 cups (200 g)

- blue M&M's® or other small blue candy

- waxed paper squares, two per child

- large spoons

- measuring cup

- two large plastic spoons

- two microwave-safe bowls

- microwave

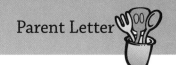

Dear Parent(s) or Guardian(s),

Today we cooked in class. Your child prepared a "Robin's Nest." Besides having fun cooking and eating, the children practiced these skills:

- listening to and following directions
- vocabulary and concept development
- measurement
- using small motor skills

For our unit *Animals Around the World*, we will send home a variety of new recipes. Each recipe will be one that your child has tried in class and is excited about. We hope you have an opportunity to try this recipe again with your child. Allowing your child to help you in the kitchen is a wonderful way to reinforce learning skills while creating family memories.

Robin's Nest

Materials

- 11.5-oz. (326 g) bag of butterscotch morsels
- 11.5-oz. (326 g) bag of chocolate morsels
- chow mein noodles, 4 cups (200 g)
- blue M&M's® or other small blue candy
- waxed paper squares
- large spoons
- measuring cup
- two large plastic spoons
- two microwave-safe bowls
- microwave

Steps to Follow

1. Measure 1 cup (200 g) of butterscotch morsels and 1 cup (200 g) of chocolate morsels and pour each into an individual microwave-safe bowl.
2. Heat both bowls of morsels for one minute. Stir the heated morsels.
3. Heat the morsels again for 15 to 30 seconds. Stir the morsels. Continue to heat and stir until the morsels are just melted.
4. Measure 2 cups (100 g) of chow mein noodles and pour them into the bowl of melted butterscotch. Stir until the noodles are completely covered.
5. Measure 2 cups (100 g) of noodles and pour them into the bowl of melted chocolate. Stir until the noodles are completely covered.
6. Use a large plastic spoon to scoop some butterscotch-covered and some chocolate-covered noodles onto a waxed paper square. This is the robin's nest.
7. Shape the nest, then add the "blue eggs."
8. Allow time for the nests to set, and enjoy!

ABC Language—Letter and Sound Recognition

Note: Children say the name of each picture aloud. Then they circle the pictures that start with the **b** sound.

Name _____

Listen for the Sound of b

Color pictures that start with the same sound as **bear**.

Write.

Note: Children count the salamanders, bears, moose, and robins. Then they write the numbers in the boxes.

Math—Counting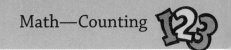

Name _____

Animal Count

Count the animals.

How many?

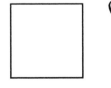 

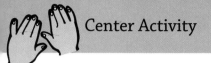

Forest Animal Puzzles

Creating the Center

1. Laminate and cut apart pages 81 and 83.

2. Place each puzzle in its own envelope. Label the outside of the envelope.

3. Place the puzzle envelopes in a sturdy folder or box with a lid.

4. Plan time to model how the center is used.

Using the Center

1. Children go to the center individually or with a partner.

2. They put together one or more of the puzzles.

3. Then children turn the puzzle pieces over to self-check their answers.

Working independently or in pairs, children put together forest animal puzzles.

Materials

- pages 81–84, laminated

- sturdy folder or box with a lid

- envelopes

- scissors

- glue

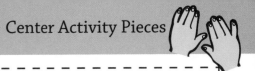

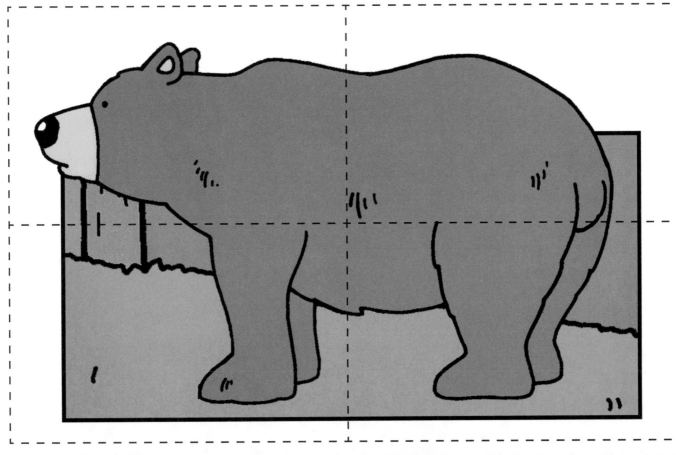

deer

Forest Animal Puzzles

bear

Forest Animal Puzzles

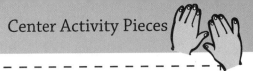

moose

Forest Animal Puzzles

©2005 by Evan-Moor Corp.
All About Animals Around the World • EMC 2411

beaver

Forest Animal Puzzles

©2005 by Evan-Moor Corp.
All About Animals Around the World • EMC 2411

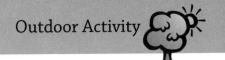
Children have fun pretending to be big bears that run from fast little bees!

Bear, Bear, Bee!

Preparation

1. Explain to children that this game is played just like Duck, Duck, Goose, but in this game, a bear runs from a bee.

2. Plan to play in an outdoor space.

How to Play

1. Children sit in a circle with their legs crossed.

2. Select one child to be the "bear." The bear walks around the circle and lightly touches each person on the head saying, "bear, bear" until he or she chooses a person to be the "bee."

3. The bee jumps up and runs in the opposite direction from the bear. Both try to reach the bee's former place in the circle first.

4. The last one to reach the empty place in the circle begins the game again by repeating steps 2 and 3.

Big Bear Chant

Big bear, big bear,
Hunting near the trees.
Feasting on the honeycomb
Made by busy bees.

Big bear, big bear,
Wading in the lake.
Fish is your favorite dish.
Which one will you take?

Big bear, big bear,
Resting in your den.
Sleeping through the winter
Before you're out again.

Note: Lead the children in holding up their fingers as they recite the rhyme.

Music/Dramatic Play Activity

Five Little Bears

One little bear
Wondering what to do.
Along came another,
Then there were two.

Two little bears
Climbing up a tree.
Along came another,
Then there were three.

Three little bears
Ate an apple core.
Along came another,
Then there were four.

Four little bears
Found honey in a hive.
Along came another,
Then there were five.

Five little bears
heard a loud roar.
One ran away,
Then there were four.

Four little bears
Climbing up a tree.
One slid down,
Then there were three.

Three little bears
Deciding what to do.
One fell asleep,
Then there were two.

Two little bears
Having lots of fun.
One went home,
Then there was one.

One little bear
Feeling all alone.
Ran to his mother,
Then there were none.

Animals of the Desert

Children learn about some of the animals that live in a desert.
Explain to children that there are many deserts all over the world.
Tell them that a desert is a place that does not have very many plants.
Explain that it does not rain very much in a desert and the weather is
very hot and dry. Explain to children that they will learn about
some of the animals that live in a desert.

All About Animals Around the World • EMC 2411 • ©2005 by Evan-Moor Corp.

Animals of the Desert

Take a walk through the desert.
Follow me.
There are many animals for us to see.

See the bobcat
sleeping during the day.
At night, it wakes up
and goes off to hunt prey.

See the speedy roadrunners
moving so fast.
You better look quickly
before they go past.

See the coyotes
walking in a pack.
They hunt at night
when the sky is black.

See the rattlesnake
sunning on a rock.
Be very quiet and still…
Shh, don't talk.

See the desert iguana
eating a flower.
It can sit in the sun
hour after hour.

See the kangaroo rat
hopping by.
Its long hind legs
help it to jump high.

Can you name the animals we saw today?
What makes the desert a good place
for them to stay?

The End

Note: Teachers will make copies
and cut them in half for minibooks.

Reproducible Story

Animals of the Desert

Take a walk through
the desert.
Follow me.
There are many animals
for us to see.

1

See the bobcat sleeping
during the day.
At night, it wakes up and
goes off to hunt prey.

2

See the speedy
roadrunners
moving so fast.
You better look
quickly before
they go past.

3

See the coyotes
walking in a pack.
They hunt at night
when the sky is black.

4

See the rattlesnake
sunning on a rock.
Be very quiet and still…
Shh, don't talk.

5

See the desert iguana
eating a flower.
It can sit in the sun
hour after hour.

6

See the kangaroo rat
hopping by.
Its long hind legs
help it to jump high.

7

Can you name
the animals
we saw today?
What makes the
desert a good place
for them to stay?

8

The End

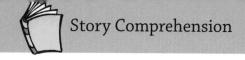
Note: Children color the animals that live in the desert.

Name _____

Who Lives in the Desert?

Color the animals that live in the desert.

Note: See page 8 for suggestions on using the storyboard pieces on pages 105 and 107 for Animals of the Desert.

Storyboard Pieces

Animals of the Desert

©2005 by Evan-Moor Corp.
All About Animals Around the World • EMC 2411

Animals of the Desert

©2005 by Evan-Moor Corp.
All About Animals Around the World
EMC 2411

Animals
of the Desert

©2005 by Evan-Moor Corp.
All About Animals Around the World
EMC 2411

Animals of the Desert

©2005 by Evan-Moor Corp.
All About Animals Around the World • EMC 2411

Children color, cut out, and glue pictures to create a desert scene.

Materials

- pages 110 and 111, reproduced, one per child
- construction paper (in desert colors), one sheet per child
- glue/water mixture
- large paintbrushes
- scissors
- crayons and markers
- sand
- newspaper

Desert Scene

Preparation

1. Discuss what a desert environment looks like. Talk about the animals shown in "Animals of the Desert" circle-time story.

2. Lay newspaper out on a table to catch the sand children sift off their papers.

Steps to Follow

1. Children brush the glue/water mixture along the bottom of the construction paper. Then they pour sand onto the glue and sift any loose sand onto a table covered with newspaper. This is their desert.

2. Then children color, cut out, and glue the animals and cactuses to their desert to complete the scene.

Note: Reproduce the patterns on pages 110 and 111 to use with Desert Scene art activity.

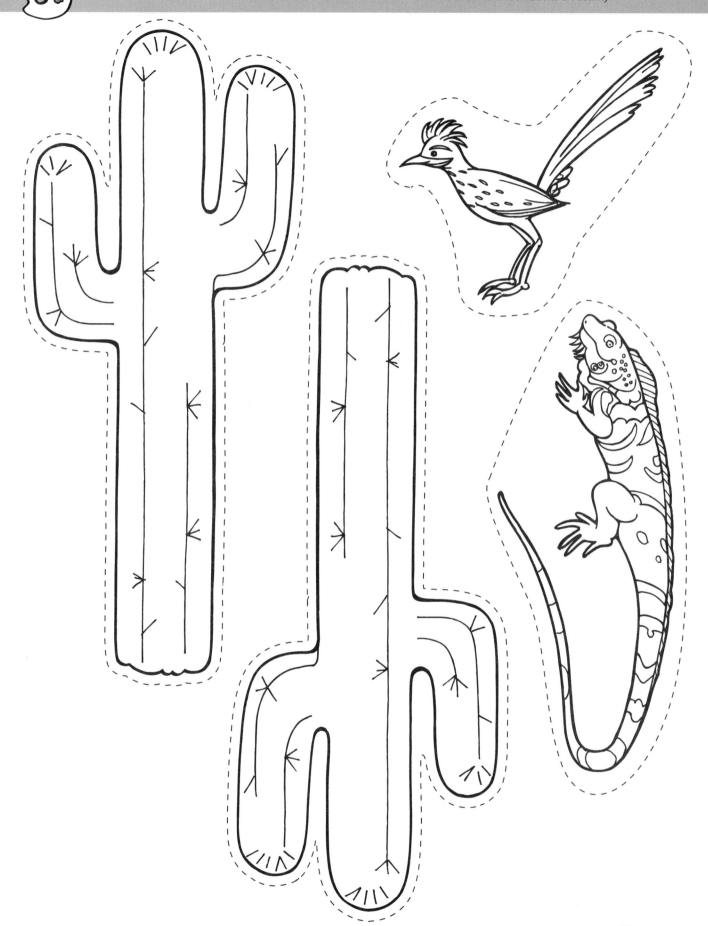

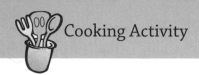
Note: Check for allergies before beginning any cooking activity. An allergic reaction can occur through taste, smell, or contact with allergens.

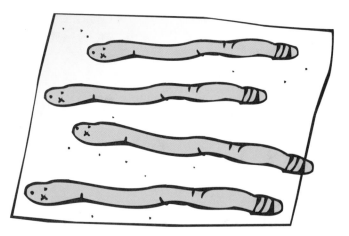

Children make breadsticks shaped like snakes with rattles on their tails!

Snake Sticks

Preparation

1. Prepare a cooking center with all materials assembled.
2. Cover a table with waxed paper.
3. Spray baking sheets with nonstick baking spray.
4. Divide the biscuit dough into a portion for each child.
5. Melt butter in a bowl. Children will dip their snake into the butter before placing it on the baking sheet.
6. Explain to children that they will make snakes out of dough.

Steps to Follow

1. Each child takes a portion of dough and rolls it into a snake shape.
2. Then children use a toothpick to make eyes and rattle marks on the snake.
3. Children dip their snake into the melted butter and lay it on the baking sheet.
4. An adult bakes the "snakes" according to the directions on the biscuit package.
5. Read a book about snakes to children while they enjoy eating their "Snake Sticks."

Materials

- refrigerated biscuit dough
- melted butter
- baking sheets
- waxed paper
- toothpicks
- small bowls to hold melted butter
- microwave or oven
- nonstick baking spray

Dear Parent(s) or Guardian(s),

Today we cooked in class. Your child prepared "Snake Sticks." Besides having fun cooking and eating, the children practiced these skills:

- listening to and following directions
- vocabulary and concept development
- using small motor skills

For our unit *Animals Around the World*, we will send home a variety of new recipes. Each recipe will be one that your child has tried in class and is excited about. We hope you have an opportunity to try this recipe again with your child. Allowing your child to help you in the kitchen is a wonderful way to reinforce learning skills while creating family memories.

Snake Sticks

Materials

- refrigerated biscuit dough
- melted butter
- baking sheets
- waxed paper
- toothpicks
- small bowl to hold melted butter
- nonstick baking spray

Steps to Follow

1. Cover a table with waxed paper.
2. Spray a baking sheet with nonstick baking spray.
3. Divide the biscuit dough into portions.
4. Melt butter in a bowl. You will dip your "snake" into the butter before placing it on the baking sheet.
5. Take a portion of dough and roll it into a snake shape.
6. Then, use a toothpick to make eyes and rattle marks on the snake.
7. Dip the snake into the melted butter and lay it on the baking sheet.
8. Bake the snakes according to the directions on the biscuit package.
9. Read aloud a book about snakes while you enjoy eating the "Snake Sticks."

ABC Language—Rhyming Words

Note: Children say the name of the first picture in each row, and then color the picture that rhymes with it.

Name _____

It's Fun to Rhyme

bug  rug

Color the picture that rhymes with the first picture in each row.

Note: Review patterning with children.
Discuss AB, AABB, and ABB patterns.

Math—Patterning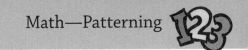

Name _____

Snake or Iguana?

Cut and glue.

Finish each pattern.

snake	iguana	snake	glue	snake	glue
snake	snake	iguana	iguana	glue	glue
snake	iguana	iguana	snake	glue	glue

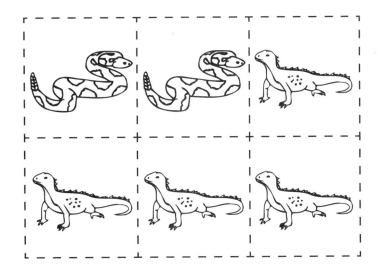

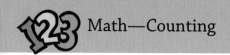

Note: Children count the bobcats and write the number on the line. Then they color the row with the most bobcats.

Name _____

How Many?

Count the bobcats. Write how many.
Color the row with the most bobcats.

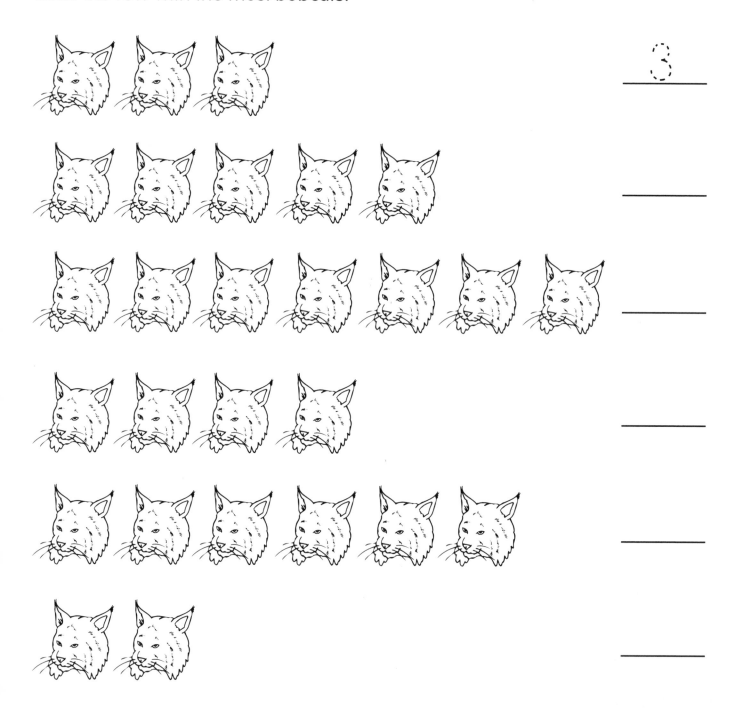

Children make a pattern with colorful snakes.

Materials

- page 118, reproduced, one per child

- pages 119 and 121, laminated

- sturdy envelope or folder

- crayons

Patterning Snakes

Creating the Center

1. Laminate and cut apart pages 119 and 121.

2. Reproduce the record form on page 118 and keep several copies at the center.

3. Place crayons at the center.

4. Review AB, AABB, AAB, and ABB patterns and plan time to model how the center is used.

Using the Center

1. Children place the snakes in patterns.

2. Children complete the record form on page 118.

Name _____

I Can Make Patterns

Color to show the snake patterns you made.

1. A B

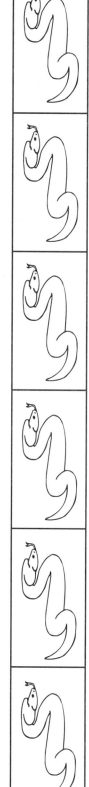

2. A A B B

3. A A B

4. A B B

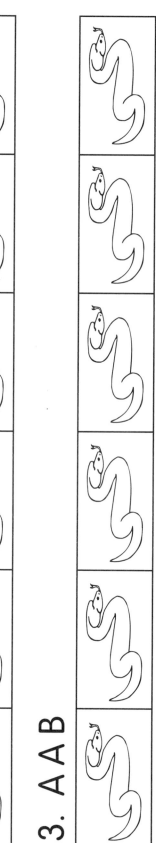

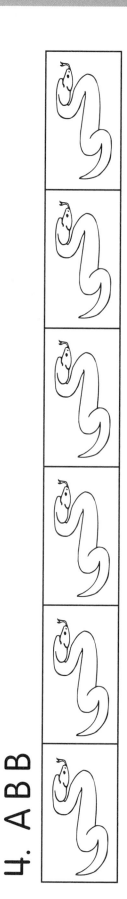

Patterning Snakes

©2005 by Evan-Moor Corp.
All About Animals Around the World • EMC 2411

Patterning Snakes

©2005 by Evan-Moor Corp.
All About Animals Around the World • EMC 2411

Patterning Snakes

©2005 by Evan-Moor Corp.
All About Animals Around the World • EMC 2411

Patterning Snakes

©2005 by Evan-Moor Corp.
All About Animals Around the World • EMC 2411

Patterning Snakes

©2005 by Evan-Moor Corp.
All About Animals Around the World • EMC 2411

Patterning Snakes

©2005 by Evan-Moor Corp.
All About Animals Around the World • EMC 2411

Patterning Snakes

©2005 by Evan-Moor Corp.
All About Animals Around the World • EMC 2411

Patterning Snakes

©2005 by Evan-Moor Corp.
All About Animals Around the World • EMC 2411

Patterning Snakes

©2005 by Evan-Moor Corp.
All About Animals Around the World • EMC 2411

Patterning Snakes

©2005 by Evan-Moor Corp.
All About Animals Around the World • EMC 2411

Patterning Snakes

©2005 by Evan-Moor Corp.
All About Animals Around the World • EMC 2411

Patterning Snakes

©2005 by Evan-Moor Corp.
All About Animals Around the World • EMC 2411

Patterning Snakes

©2005 by Evan-Moor Corp.
All About Animals Around the World • EMC 2411

Patterning Snakes

©2005 by Evan-Moor Corp.
All About Animals Around the World • EMC 2411

Patterning Snakes

©2005 by Evan-Moor Corp.
All About Animals Around the World • EMC 2411

Patterning Snakes

©2005 by Evan-Moor Corp.
All About Animals Around the World • EMC 2411

Children run as fast as a roadrunner to the finish line!

Roadrunner Races

Preparation

1. Plan to play this game in a grassy area outdoors.

2. Use cones, flags, or rope to mark a start line and a finish line.

3. Explain to children that roadrunners are very fast birds! They can run at speeds of up to 17 miles per hour. Tell children that roadrunners prefer to run rather than fly. Explain that they will run a race as fast as they can—just like a roadrunner!

How to Play

1. Divide the class into two lines. Children line up behind the start line.

2. The first child in each line stands at the start line. The teacher says, *1, 2, 3—GO!* Both children race to the finish line as fast as they can.

3. Continue play until all the children have had a turn to race.

Extension

Ask a couple of adults to stand at the finish line with a stopwatch. Have the adults announce each child's time as he or she finishes the race.

All the Bobcats Chant

All the bobcats fast asleep.

All the bobcats not a peep.

If I should sing my song today,

Will all those bobcats get up and play?
(Children get up and move around the room
on all fours.)

Get up, little bobcats, walk around.

Get up, little bobcats, make a sound.
(Children make bobcat sounds.)

Get up, little bobcats, move your paws.
(Children move their hands.)

Get up, little bobcats, show your claws!
(Children get up on their knees, hold up their hands,
and "show their claws.")

Extension

Substitute different animals in this rhyme.

Children begin by lying
on the floor, pretending
to be sleeping bobcats.

Children imitate desert animals while singing this interactive song.

Down in the Desert Chant

Preparation

1. Children sit in rows. The teacher sits in front of the class and leads them in singing this interactive rhyme.

2. Each time the teacher says an animal name, the first child in the row hops, walks, or runs (whatever action the teacher said) past the group of children and then goes to the end of the row. Repeat until each child has had a turn.

   Teacher:
   Down in the desert where the cactuses grow,
   A rattlesnake slithered by, and I said…
   (The first child in line slithers past the group and then goes to the end of the row.)

   Class:
   Whoa!

Repeat

Down in the desert where the cactuses grow, a kangaroo rat hopped by, and I said Whoa!

Down in the desert where the cactuses grow, a bobcat ran by, and I said Whoa!

Down in the desert where the cactuses grow, a desert iguana scurried by, and I said Whoa!

Down in the desert where the cactuses grow, a roadrunner ran by, and I said Whoa!

Down in the desert where the cactuses grow, a coyote trotted by, and I said Whoa!

Animals of the Arctic Tundra

Children learn about some of the animals that live in the Arctic tundra. Explain to children that the area of land called the "Arctic tundra" is at the top of the world around the North Pole. It is like a cold desert with a layer of permanently frozen soil in the ground. Explain to children that they will learn about some of the animals that live in the Arctic tundra.

Animals of the Arctic Tundra

Take a walk through the Arctic tundra.
Follow me.
There are many animals for us to see.

See the arctic fox with the long tail
and four furry feet.
It walks across the tundra
looking for something to eat.

See the arctic hare
camouflaged in the snow.
It stays very still
so predators will not know!

See the white snowy owl
with bright yellow eyes.
It hunts at night,
flying silently through the skies.

See the seals slide
across the ice—1, 2, 3.
Plunk! They dive into
the cold blue Arctic Sea.

See the herd of caribou "shoveling" snow.
They dig with their antlers
to find the grass below.

See the blubbery walrus
using its tusks to climb up.
Hey, look right behind it.
There's a walrus pup!

 All About Animals Around the World • EMC 2411 • ©2005 by Evan-Moor Corp.

Tell me about the wild animals
we have seen today.
What makes the Arctic tundra
a good place for them to stay?

The End

Animals of the Arctic Tundra

Take a walk through the
Arctic tundra.
Follow me.
There are many animals
for us to see.

1

See the arctic fox
with the long tail
and four furry feet.
It walks across the
tundra looking for
something to eat.

2

See the arctic hare
camouflaged in the snow.
It stays very still so
predators will not know!

3

See the white snowy owl with bright yellow eyes. It hunts at night, flying silently through the skies.

4

See the seals slide across the ice—1, 2, 3. Plunk! They dive into the cold blue Arctic Sea.

5

See the herd of caribou "shoveling" snow.
They dig with their antlers to find the grass below.

6

See the blubbery walrus using its tusks to climb up.
Hey, look right behind it.
There's a walrus pup!

7

Tell me about the wild animals we have seen today. What makes the Arctic tundra a good place for them to stay?

8

The End

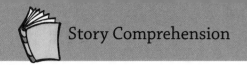

Story Comprehension

Note: Review the animals that live in the Arctic tundra. Children find and color the animals presented in Animals of the Arctic Tundra circle-time story.

Name _____

I Live Here

Color the animals that live in the Arctic tundra.

Note: See page 8 for suggestions on using the storyboard pieces on pages 143 and 145 for Animals of the Arctic Tundra.

Storyboard Pieces

Animals of the
Arctic Tundra

©2005 by Evan-Moor Corp.
All About Animals Around the World • EMC 2411

Animals of the
Arctic Tundra

©2005 by Evan-Moor Corp.
All About Animals Around the World • EMC 2411

Animals of the
Arctic Tundra

©2005 by Evan-Moor Corp.
All About Animals Around the World • EMC 2411

Animals of the
Arctic Tundra

©2005 by Evan-Moor Corp.
All About Animals Around the World • EMC 2411

Animals of the
Arctic Tundra

©2005 by Evan-Moor Corp.
All About Animals Around the World • EMC 2411

Animals of the
Arctic Tundra

©2005 by Evan-Moor Corp.
All About Animals Around the World • EMC 2411

Animals of the
Arctic Tundra

©2005 by Evan-Moor Corp.
All About Animals Around the World
EMC 2411

Animals of the
Arctic Tundra

©2005 by Evan-Moor Corp.
All About Animals Around the World • EMC 2411

Cornstarch Clay Walrus

Children make cornstarch clay and shape it into an arctic walrus.

Materials

Ingredients for 20 to 30 walruses:

- 2 cups (250 g) cornstarch
- 4 cups (500 g) baking soda
- 2⅔ (236 mL) cups water
- saucepan
- stove top or hotplate
- spoon
- cutting board
- gray and black tempera paint
- paintbrushes
- pencils
- broom straws
- white pipe cleaner

Preparation

1. Prepare a cooking center and an art center with all materials assembled.
2. Cut the pipe cleaner into short tusks.
3. Decide which clay-making tasks are appropriate for your class. Allow children to participate where appropriate.

Steps to Follow

Making the clay:

1. Pour the water into a pan. Stir over medium heat as you add the cornstarch and baking soda. When the mixture is like mashed potatoes, remove it from heat.
2. Pour the mixture onto a cutting board to cool. As soon as the dough is cool enough, knead it.
3. Roll a 3" (7.5 cm) diameter ball of clay for each child. Keep the clay in an airtight container until you are ready to complete the project. The clay will keep for several weeks.
4. Plan time to model the steps for this project and a completed Cornstarch Clay Walrus.

Making the walrus:

1. Children take a 3" (7.5 cm) diameter ball of clay and shape it into a log-like shape, but with a rounded top and a flat bottom.
2. Then they use a pencil to draw a walrus muzzle on one end of the clay. Children poke pieces of broom straw into the muzzle for whiskers, and then use a pencil to add nose holes and eyes.
3. They push a white piece of pipe cleaner into each side of the muzzle for the tusks.
4. Children air dry the walruses until they are hard.
5. Once the walruses have hardened, children paint the body gray and the eyes and nose holes black. They also paint the tips of the broom straw black.

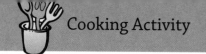

Note: Check for allergies before beginning any cooking activity. An allergic reaction can occur through taste, smell, or contact with allergens.

Arctic Hare Cookies

Children will enjoy creating these yummy arctic hare cookies!

Preparation

1. Determine how many refrigerated cookie dough rolls and frosting tubs your class will need in order for each child to make two cookies. Place waxed paper on a table and sprinkle flour onto the paper.

2. Preheat the oven as directed on the cookie dough package.

3. Allow children to share what they know about arctic hares. Tell them that it is hard to tell the difference between a rabbit and a hare. Explain to children that hares are usually larger and have longer ears.

Steps to Follow

1. Children roll out the cookie dough onto floured waxed paper and use a rabbit-shaped cookie cutter to make two arctic hare cookie shapes.

2. They use a floured spatula to place their cookies onto a cookie sheet.

3. An adult bakes the cookies as directed on the package, and allows time for them to cool before allowing children to frost them.

4. Children spread vanilla frosting on their arctic hares. They may sprinkle coconut on the tails. Then they use colored decorating gel to make the eyes and whiskers.

5. Enjoy!

Materials

- refrigerated sugar cookie-dough roll
- vanilla frosting
- colored decorating gel
- coconut
- flour
- rolling pins
- spatula
- rabbit-shaped cookie cutters
- cookie sheets
- waxed paper
- oven
- dull plastic knives (adult supervision)

Dear Parent(s) or Guardian(s),

Today we cooked in class. Your child prepared "Arctic Hare Cookies." Besides having fun cooking and eating, the children practiced these skills:

- listening to and following directions
- vocabulary and concept development
- using small motor skills

For our unit *Animals Around the World,* we will send home a variety of new recipes. Each recipe will be one that your child has tried in class and is excited about. We hope you have an opportunity to try this recipe again with your child. Allowing your child to help you in the kitchen is a wonderful way to reinforce learning skills while creating family memories.

Arctic Hare Cookies

Materials

- refrigerated sugar cookie-dough roll
- vanilla frosting
- colored decorating gel
- coconut
- flour
- rolling pin
- spatula
- rabbit-shaped cookie cutter
- cookie sheet
- waxed paper
- plastic knife

Steps to Follow

1. Roll out the cookie dough onto floured waxed paper and use a rabbit-shaped cookie cutter to make arctic hare cookie shapes.

2. Use a floured spatula to place cookies onto a cookie sheet.

3. An adult bakes the cookies as directed on the package, and allows time for them to cool.

4. Use vanilla frosting to decorate the arctic hares. Sprinkle coconut on the tails, and use colored decorating gel to make the eyes and whiskers.

5. Enjoy!

Name _____

Above and Below

Listen and do.

1. Draw a circle above the fox.
2. Write an **X** below the snowy owl.
3. Draw a circle above the arctic hare.
4. Write an **X** below the seal.
5. Draw the sun above the snowy owl.

Note: Children add the foxes in each box and then write the sum on the line.

Name _____

How Many Foxes?

| 1 | 2 | 3 | 4 | 5 | 6 | 7 | 8 | 9 | 10 |

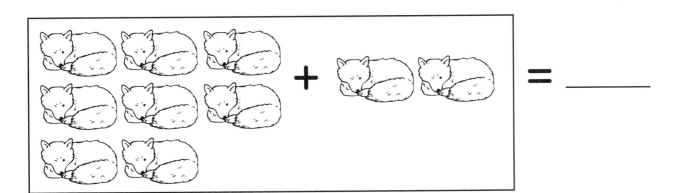

= _____

= _____

= _____

= _____

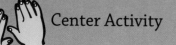

Children match up an arctic animal picture with a picture of a magnified part of the same animal.

Materials

- pages 153 and 155, laminated
- magnifying glass
- small sturdy bag

Animals Magnified

Creating the Center

1. Laminate and cut out pages 153 and 155. Store the cards in a small sturdy bag.

2. Place the Animals of the Arctic Tundra circle-time story at the center. Demonstrate for the children how to look at pictures using a magnifying glass. Discuss how animal parts look larger with the magnifier.

3. Plan time to model how the center is used.

Using the Center

1. Player 1 selects two cards from the bag. He or she looks at the cards and checks to see if they show a full-size animal and a magnified part of the same animal.

2. If the picture cards show the same animal, then the player keeps them. If they do not match, both picture cards are returned to the bag.

3. Player 2 repeats the same process.

4. The game is played until all the animal cards have been matched with their magnified parts.

Animals Magnified

©2005 by Evan-Moor Corp.
All About Animals Around the World • EMC 2411

Animals Magnified

©2005 by Evan-Moor Corp.
All About Animals Around the World • EMC 2411

Animals Magnified

©2005 by Evan-Moor Corp.
All About Animals Around the World • EMC 2411

Animals Magnified

©2005 by Evan-Moor Corp.
All About Animals Around the World • EMC 2411

Animals Magnified

©2005 by Evan-Moor Corp.
All About Animals Around the World • EMC 2411

Animals Magnified

©2005 by Evan-Moor Corp.
All About Animals Around the World • EMC 2411

Animals Magnified

Animals Magnified

Animals Magnified

Animals Magnified

Animals Magnified

Animals Magnified

Children pass around a large and a small ball, pretending they are a fox chasing a hare.

Materials

- small ball
- large ball

Catch the Hare

How to Play

1. Children sit or stand in a circle.

2. They pass the "hare" (small ball) around the circle in one direction.

3. Once the hare is about halfway around, the "fox" (large ball) is passed around the circle in the same direction. The fox tries to catch the hare. The fox can be passed in either direction and can change directions at any time.

4. The object of the game is for the fox to catch the hare.

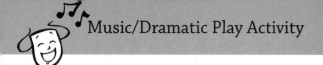

Note: Make the snowy owl finger puppets on page 159 for children to wear while performing this finger play.

Five Snowy Owls

Children perform a counting finger play.

Five snowy owls
perched near the shore.

One flew away and
then there were four.

Four snowy owls
perched in a tree.

One flew away and
then there were three.

Three snowy owls
singing hoo hoo,

One flew away and
then there were two.

Two snowy owls
sitting in the sun,

One flew away and
then there was one.

One snowy owl
flying up so high,

Soaring through the bright sky.

Note: Reproduce these patterns for children. Each child will color, cut out, and tape five owl finger puppets.

Music/Dramatic Play Pattern Pieces

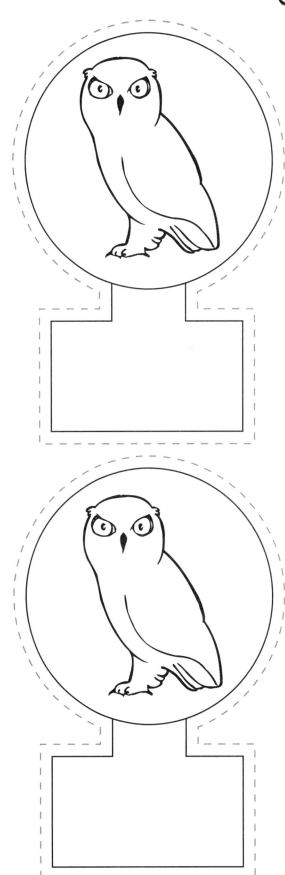

Animals of the Rainforest

Children learn about some of the animals that live in a South American rainforest. Explain to children that there are several rainforests. Tell them that rainforests are wet places that get a lot of rain, sunlight, and warmth. Explain to them that rainforests have many plants, bushes, and trees. Tell children that they will learn about some of the animals that live in a South American rainforest.

Animals of the Rainforest

Take a walk through the rainforest.
Follow me.
There are many animals for us to see.

1

See the giant anteater
standing near the plants.
It is looking for its food—
termites and ants!

See the jaguar
standing way up high.
It watches the birds
as they fly by.

3

See the sloth
hanging from the tree.
Its body moves
very slo-o-o-wly.

4

See the spider monkey
moving through the trees.
It uses its arms, legs, and tail
to swing with ease.

See the toucan's beak.
It's red, orange, and green.
It's the most colorful bird
I've ever seen!

See the harpy eagle
flying through the trees.
It spreads its large wings
and glides on the breeze.

Tell me the animals
we have seen today.
What makes the rainforest
a good place for them to stay?

8

The End

Note: Teachers will make copies
and cut them in half for minibooks.

Reproducible Story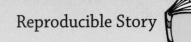

Animals of the Rainforest

Take a walk through the
rainforest.
Follow me.
There are many animals
for us to see.

1

See the giant anteater standing near the plants. It is looking for its food— termites and ants!

2

See the jaguar standing way up high. It watches the birds as they fly by.

3

See the sloth
hanging from the tree.
Its body moves
very slo-o-o-wly.

4

See the spider monkey
moving through the trees.
It uses its arms, legs, and
tail to swing with ease.

5

Animals of the Rainforest

See the toucan's beak.
It's red, orange, and green.
It's the most colorful
bird I've ever seen!

6

See the harpy eagle
flying through the trees.
It spreads its large wings
and glides on the breeze.

7

Tell me the animals we have seen today. What makes the rainforest a good place for them to stay?

8

The End

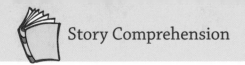

Story Comprehension

Note: Explain to children that they circle the animals that belong in the rainforest and write an **X** on the animals that do <u>not</u> belong.

Name _____

Which Animals Belong?

Which animals belong in the rainforest?

Circle the animals that belong.

Write an **X** on the animals that do <u>not</u> belong.

Note: See page 9 for suggestions on using the storyboard pieces on pages 177 and 179 for Animals of the Rainforest.

Storyboard Pieces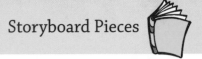

Animals
of the Rainforest

©2005 by Evan-Moor Corp.
All About Animals Around the World • EMC 2411

Animals
of the Rainforest

©2005 by Evan-Moor Corp.
All About Animals Around the World • EMC 2411

Animals
of the Rainforest

©2005 by Evan-Moor Corp.
All About Animals Around the World • EMC 2411

Animals
of the Rainforest

©2005 by Evan-Moor Corp.
All About Animals Around the World
EMC 2411

Animals
of the Rainforest

©2005 by Evan-Moor Corp.
All About Animals Around the World • EMC 2411

Animals
of the Rainforest

©2005 by Evan-Moor Corp.
All About Animals Around the World • EMC 2411

Animals
of the Rainforest

©2005 by Evan-Moor Corp.
All About Animals Around the World • EMC 2411

Children make monkey headbands to wear while they "monkey" around.

Materials

- page 182, reproduced, one per child

- 12" x 18" (30.5 x 45.5 cm) brown construction paper strips, one per child

- scissors

- glue

- crayons or markers

- tape

Monkey Headbands

Preparation

1. Prepare an art center with all materials assembled.

2. Cut 12" x 18" (30.5 x 45.5 cm) brown construction paper into headband strips.

3. Plan time to model the steps for this project and a completed Monkey Headband.

Steps to Follow

1. Children color and cut out the monkey patterns on page 182.

2. They glue the patterns to a strip of brown construction paper.

3. Then children have an adult fit the strip to their head size and tape it together.

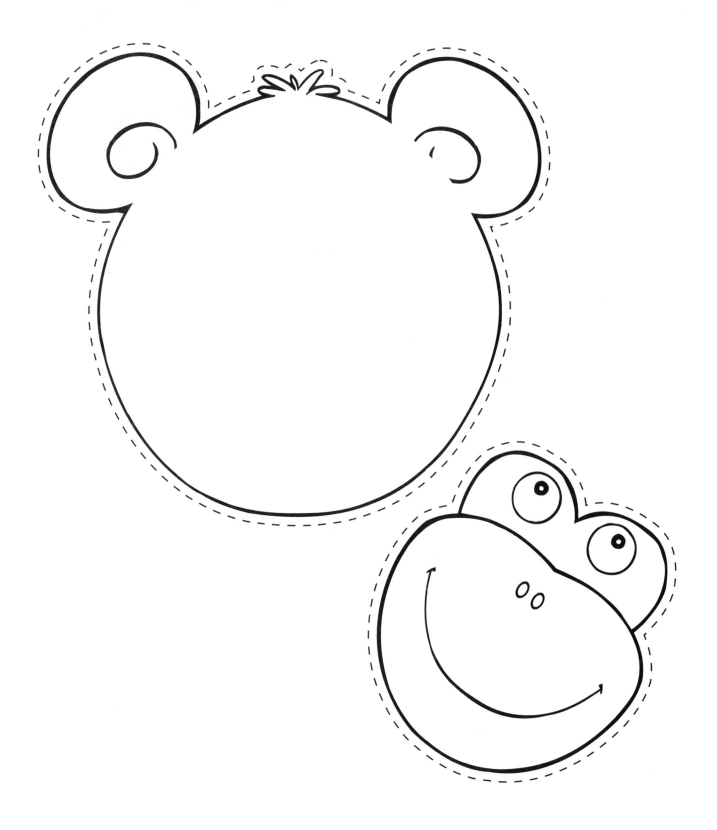

Note: Check for allergies before beginning any cooking activity.
An allergic reaction can occur through taste, smell, or contact with allergens.

Cooking Activity

Children make healthy "banana dogs" using fresh fruit and hot dog buns. Children love the taste, and you will love the fact that these are simple and quick.

Banana Dogs

Preparation

1. Prepare a cooking center with all ingredients assembled.

2. Show children the ingredients and ask them to identify each one.

3. Model how to use a plastic knife to spread the honey or peanut butter onto the hot dog bun. Model how to peel the banana and place it in the hot dog bun. Place the strawberry slices on top of the banana. Sprinkle blueberries and raspberries on the banana.

4. Tell children that bananas are one of a monkey's favorite foods. Talk about how a monkey uses its hands to eat a banana. Ask children if they have ever seen a monkey eat a banana.

Steps to Follow

1. Children take a hot dog bun and use a dull plastic knife to spread honey or peanut butter on it.

2. They peel a banana and place it in the bun.

3. Then children use a dull plastic knife to slice a strawberry (adult supervision required). They place the strawberry slices on the banana.

4. Children sprinkle blueberries and raspberries on their banana dog.

5. Children wear their monkey headbands (page 181) while enjoying their banana dog.

Extension

Try the same activity, but this time add raisins, coconut, and any other toppings you find interesting.

Materials

- bananas, one per child

- hot dog buns, one per child

- strawberry (sliced), one per child

- honey or peanut butter, 2 teaspoons (12 g) per child (allergy alert)

- blueberries and raspberries

- paper towels

- dull plastic knives (adult supervision)

Dear Parent(s) or Guardian(s),

Today we cooked in class. Your child prepared "Banana Dogs." Besides having fun cooking and eating, the children practiced these skills:

- listening to and following directions
- vocabulary and concept development
- using small motor skills

For our unit *Animals Around the World*, we will send home a variety of new recipes. Each recipe will be one that your child has tried in class and is excited about. We hope you have an opportunity to try this recipe again with your child. Allowing your child to help you in the kitchen is a wonderful way to reinforce learning skills while creating family memories.

Banana Dogs

Materials

- bananas, one per person
- hot dog buns, one per person
- strawberry (sliced), one per person
- honey or peanut butter, 2 teaspoons (12 g) per person (allergy alert)
- blueberries and raspberries
- paper towels
- dull plastic knives (adult supervision)

Steps to Follow

1. Use the knife to spread the honey or peanut butter onto the hot dog bun. Peel the banana and place it in the bun. Place the strawberry slices on top of the banana. Sprinkle blueberries and raspberries on the banana.

2. Enjoy!

Note: Discuss the positional words *above* and *below*. Use objects in your classroom as examples. Read aloud the directions below, pausing after each item to allow time for children to complete it.

Language—Positional Words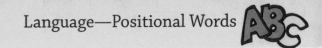

Name _____

Above the Toucan, Below the Toucan

Listen. Draw.

1. Draw a circle above the toucan sitting on the log.

2. Draw an **X** below the toucan in the tree.

3. Draw a circle above the toucan on the forest floor.

4. Draw a **X** below the toucan on the anteater's back.

Note: Children color the toucans according to the number at the left of each row.

Name _____

Toucan Count

Color the correct number of toucans.

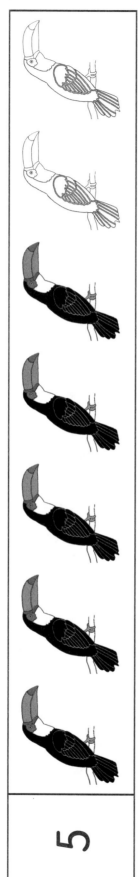

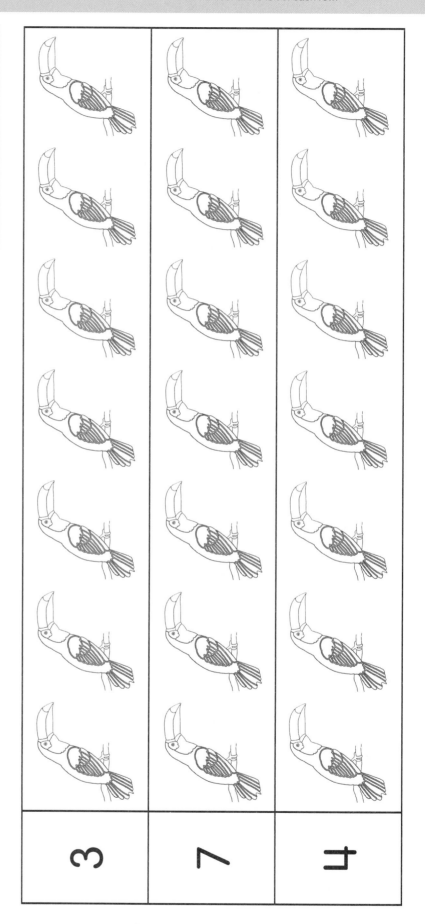

Note: Children read the number on each anteater to see how many ants it wants to eat. Then they place the correct number of ants in a trail in front of the anteater's snout.

Center Activity

Children feed ants to hungry anteaters who have requested a particular number of ants.

Materials

- page 188, reproduced 10 times and laminated

- page 189, reproduced five times and laminated

- 9" x 12" (23 x 30.5 cm) construction paper, various colors

- permanent black marker

- scissors

- sturdy folder or envelope

Hungry Anteaters

Creating the Center

1. Reproduce page 188 on colored construction paper ten times. Use a black marker to number the anteaters 1 through 10. Laminate and cut out the anteaters.

2. Reproduce page 189 five times. You need 55 ants for this center. Laminate and cut apart the ants. Place them in an envelope.

3. Store the anteaters and the envelope of ants in a sturdy folder or larger envelope.

4. Explain to children that a giant anteater uses its large strong claws to break open ant and termite nests. Then it pokes its long nose and tongue into the nest to find food. Its tongue is about a foot long and is its main source for gathering food.

5. Plan time to model how the center is used.

Using the Center

1. Children choose an anteater and place it on the table or floor.

2. They read the number on the anteater and place the correct number of ants in a trail in front of the anteater's snout.

3. Children continue to choose anteaters and lay out the correct number of ants for them to eat until all the anteaters have been fed.

Note: Reproduce this pattern to use with Hungry Anteaters center activity.

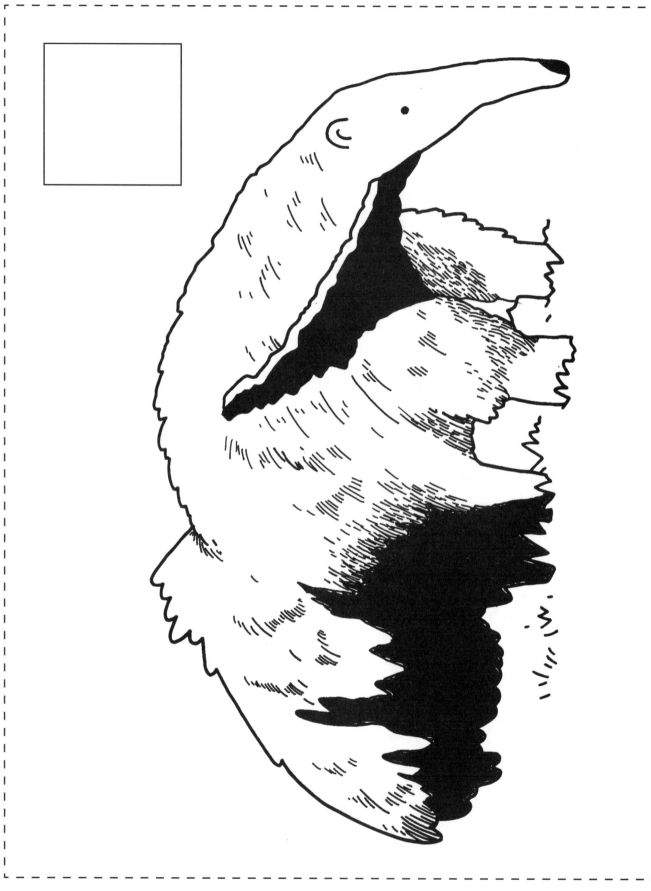

Note: Reproduce these patterns to use with Hungry Anteaters center activity.

 Outdoor Activity

Note: Discuss the different rainforest animals mentioned below. Talk about the different movements the animals use.

Walking Through the Rainforest

How to Play

1. Play this game in a large outdoor area.
2. Children move and make noises (if applicable) like each animal they sing about.

I'm walking through the rainforest,
and what do I see?

A **toucan** *sitting* in a tree.

(Children cup hands for feet.)

I'm walking through the rainforest,
and what do I see?

A **sloth** *hanging* from a tree.

I'm walking through the rainforest,
and what do I see?

A **monkey** *swinging* from tree to tree.

I'm walking through the rainforest,
and what do I see?

An **eagle** *perched* in a tree.

I'm walking through the rainforest,
and what do I see?

An **anteater** *climbing* in a tree.

I'm walking through the rainforest,
and what do I see?

A **jaguar** *leaping* from a tree.

Children sing this repetitive chant with a different animal and movement word in each verse.

Note: Before teaching children this song, discuss the four layers in a rainforest: the emergent, the canopy, the understory, and the forest floor. Talk about the different animals that inhabit each layer. Sing this song to the tune of "If You're Happy and You Know It."

Music/Dramatic Play Activity

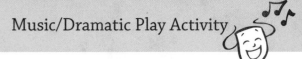

The Rainforest Song

There are layers
in the forest, yes indeed.
Yes indeed!

There are layers
in the forest, yes indeed.
Yes indeed!

The emergent, the canopy,
and the understory.
There are layers
in the forest.
Yes indeed!

The emergent is home
to birds and butterflies.
Butterflies!

The emergent is home
to birds and butterflies.
Butterflies!

The trees are so high that
they almost touch the sky.
The emergent is home
to birds and butterflies.
Butterflies!

The canopy is like
a big umbrella.
Big umbrella!

The canopy is like
a big umbrella.
Big umbrella!

Monkeys, sloth, orangutan
Eat all the fruit they can.
The canopy is like
a big umbrella.
Big umbrella!

The understory is home
to many snakes.
Many snakes!

The understory is home
to many snakes.
Many snakes!

They eat rats and bats,
And they like the
gnats for snacks.

The understory is home
to many snakes.
Many snakes!

The forest floor is dim
and dark and wet.
Dark and wet!

The forest floor is dim
and dark and wet.
Dark and wet!

The ants go marching
by as they watch the
birds up high.
The forest floor is dim
and dark and wet.
Dark and wet!

Alphabet Cards

Use these colorful Alphabet Cards in a variety of ways. Simply laminate and cut apart the cards and store them in a sturdy envelope or box.

Alphabet cards can be used to practice skills such as:

- letter recognition
- letter-sound association
- visual perception

Alphabet Card Games

What's My Name?   Use the alphabet cards to introduce the names of the letters, both uppercase and lowercase.

Make a Match   Children match a lowercase and uppercase letter. They then turn the cards over to self-check. If a correct match has been made, the child will see a picture of the same object whose name begins with the letter being matched.

First-Sound Game   Use the alphabet cards as phonics flash cards and ask children to identify the sound of each letter.

ABC Order   Children take all of the uppercase or lowercase cards and place them in alphabetical order.

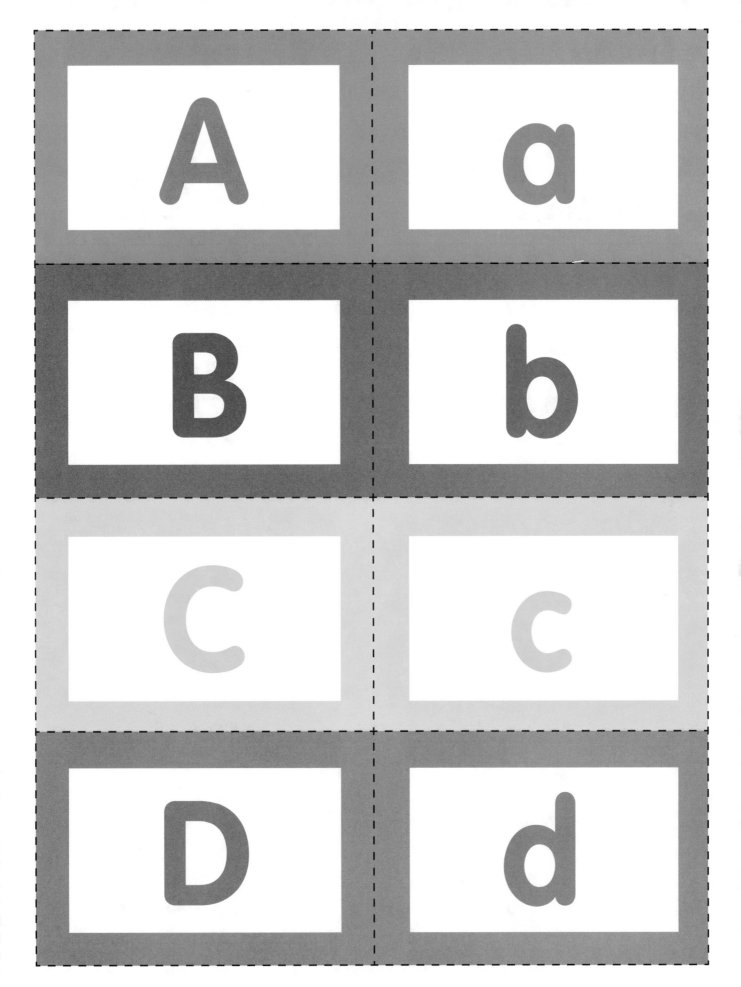

anteater

Anteater

bear

Bear

caribou

Caribou

deer

Deer

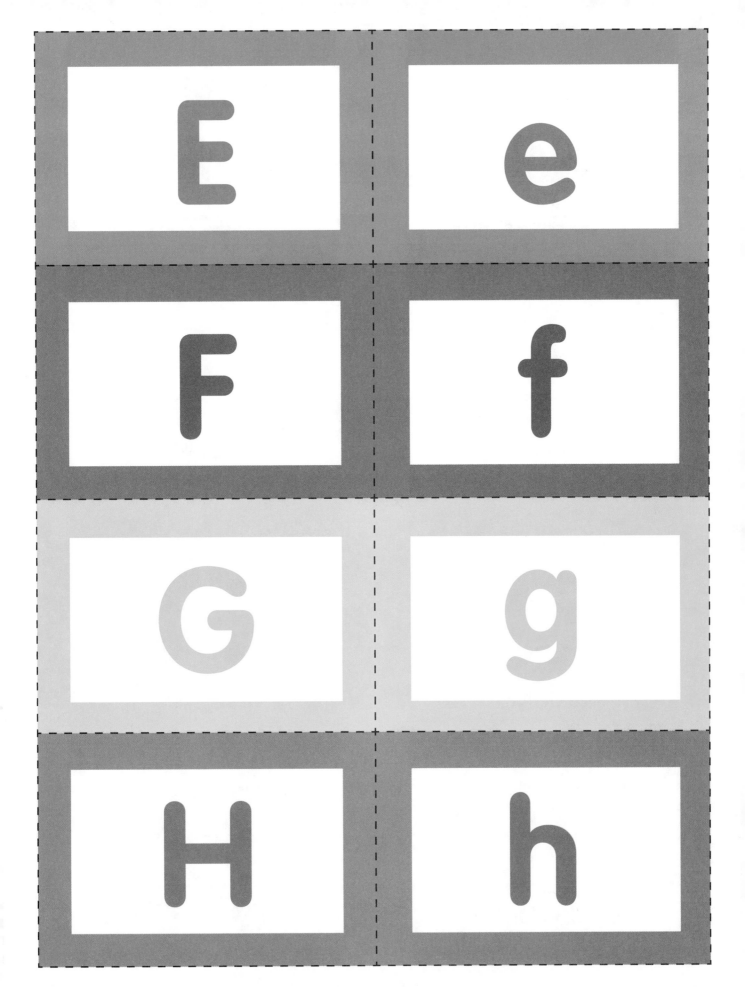

elephant

Elephant

fox

Fox

giraffe

Giraffe

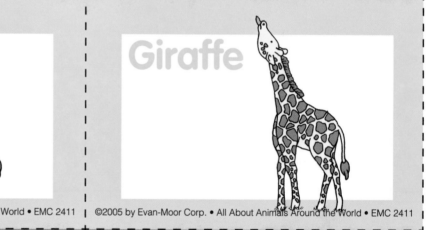

hippo

Hippo

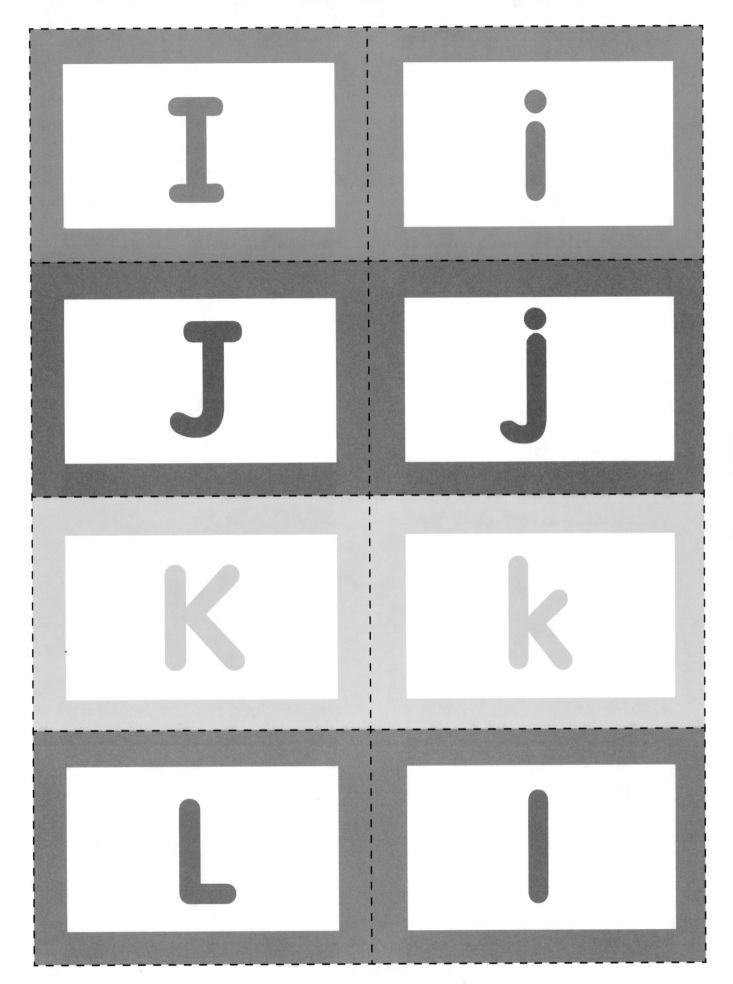

I   i

J   j

K   k

L   l

iguana

Iguana

jaguar

Jaguar

kangaroo rat

Kangaroo rat

lion

Lion

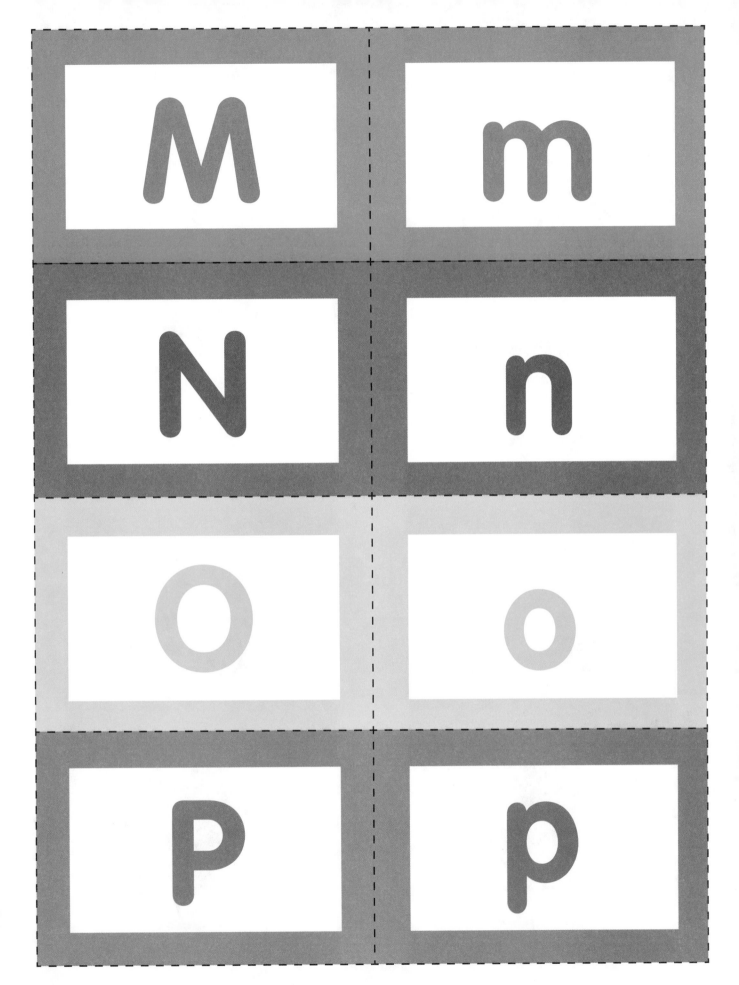

M m

N n

O o

P p

monkey

Monkey

nest

Nest

owl

Owl

plant

Plant

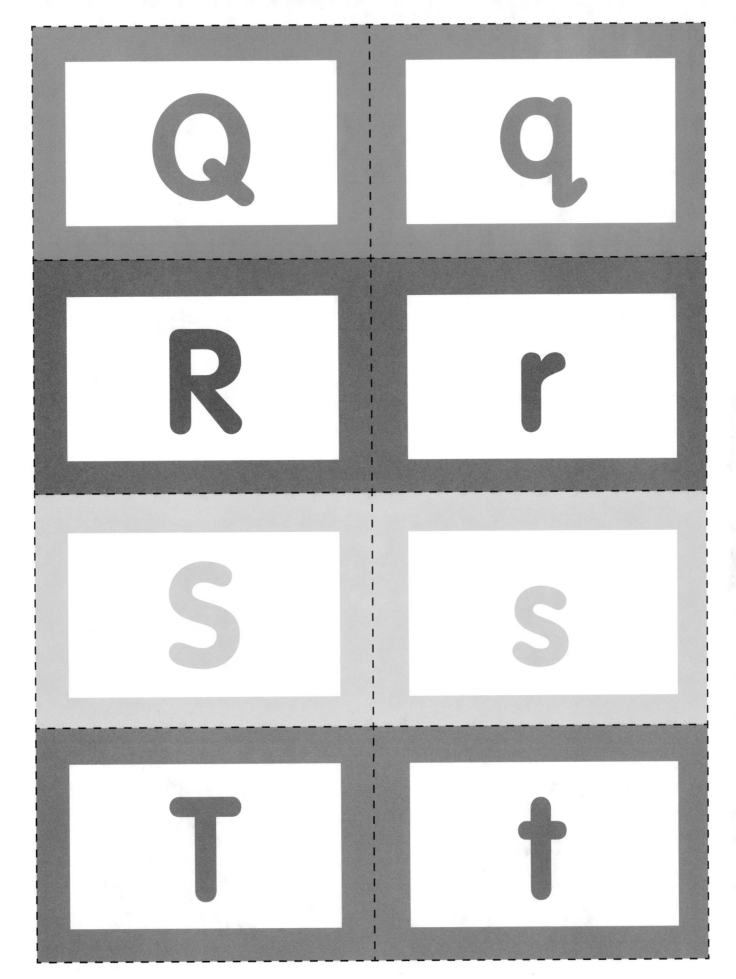

quail

Quail

roadrunner

Roadrunner

snake

Snake

toucan

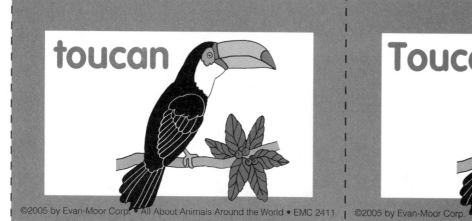

Toucan

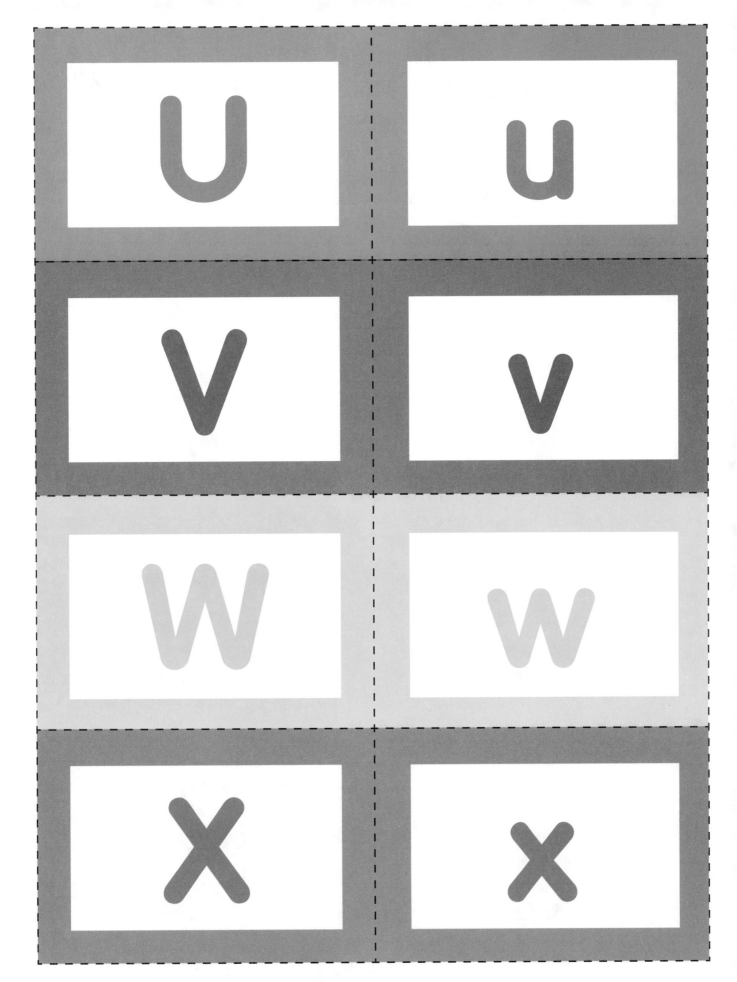

upside down

Upside down

vine

Vine

walrus

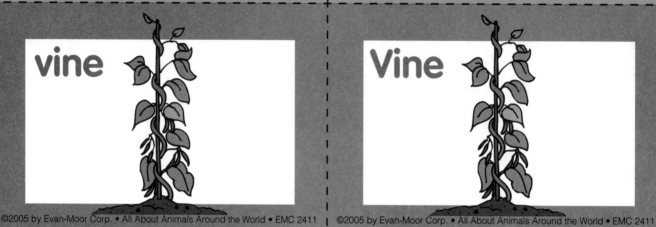

Walrus

x on a gate

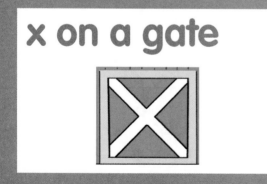

X on a gate

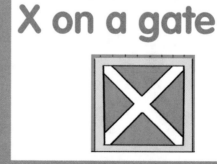

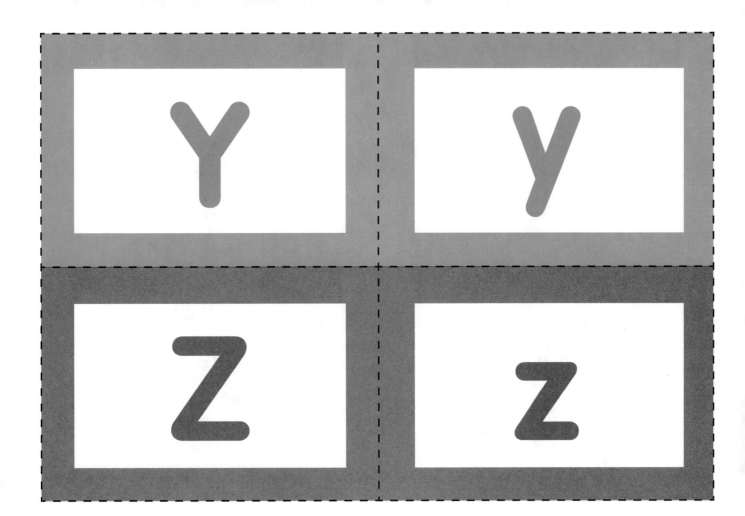

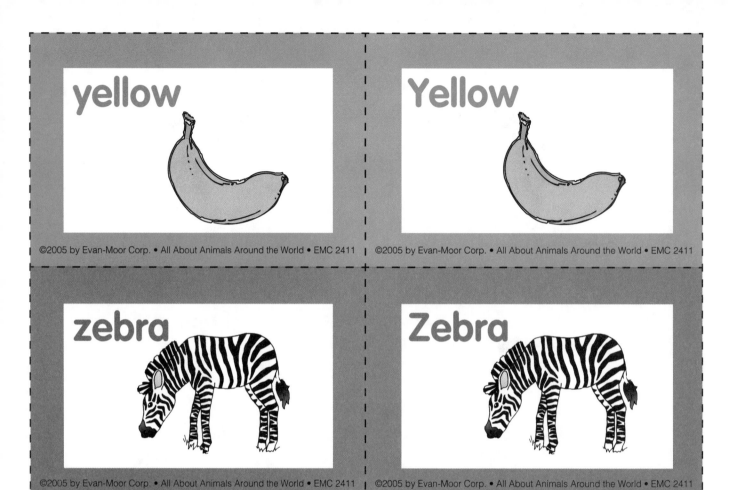

yellow

©2005 by Evan-Moor Corp. • All About Animals Around the World • EMC 2411

Yellow

©2005 by Evan-Moor Corp. • All About Animals Around the World • EMC 2411

zebra

©2005 by Evan-Moor Corp. • All About Animals Around the World • EMC 2411

Zebra

©2005 by Evan-Moor Corp. • All About Animals Around the World • EMC 2411

Answer Key

Page 28

Page 66

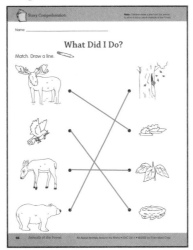

Page 104

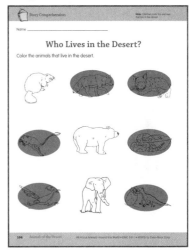

Page 38

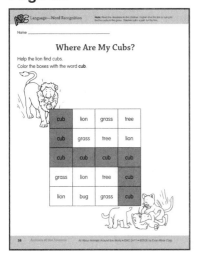

Page 78

Page 114

Page 39

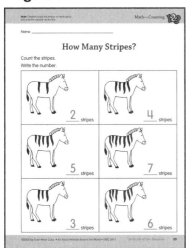

Page 79

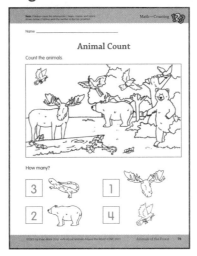

Page 115

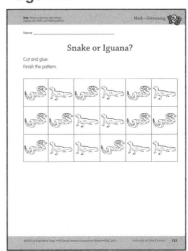

Page 116

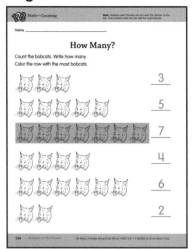

Page 150

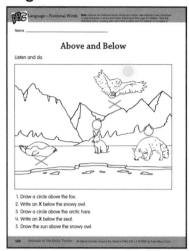

Page 185

Page 118

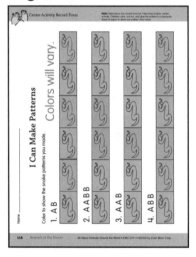

Page 151

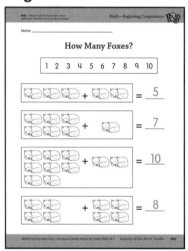

Page 186

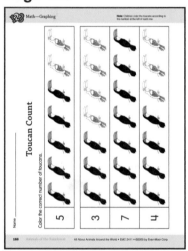

Page 142

Page 176

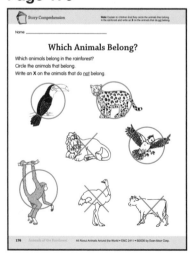